AWAKEN

Awaken
The Sleeping Be-ING

Channeled by Anna Harlas

Epigraph Books
Rhinebeck, New York

ISBN: 978-1-944037-41-3
Library of Congress Control Number: 2016951762

Book and cover design by Colin Rolfe
Buddha art by Barbara McGlynn

Printed in the United States of America.

Epigraph Books
22 East Market Street, Suite 304
Rhinebeck, NY 12572
(845) 876-4861

Contact the author:
Anna Harlas—New Paltz, New York
Email: astraanna@aol.com
Phone: (845) 255-0312 — Cell: (646) 270-0344

(The book teaches that we are the Creator of our life.
Therefore, I am dedicating the book to the reader.)

FOR THE CREATOR

TABLE OF CONTENTS

PROLOGUE
THE UNITING OF ANNA AND THE GUARDIAN ANGEL 'ASTRA'

My mother was the first to meet my Guardian Angel. I was 6 months old. She didn't tell me how this happened until I was in my twenties. As my mother spoke she began to cry, remembering that when I was born I had a mark on my forehead the size of a silver dollar. I grew older, and the mark also grew, this upset my mother, thinking my face would be covered by this birthmark.

One day, while out in the Brooklyn neighborhood where we lived, my mother was pushing my carriage when a well-dressed woman came up to her and looked into the carriage saying, "What a beautiful baby!" My mother said, "But look at the mark on her face, it has been growing larger and I am afraid it will cover her entire face."

The woman then told my mother that she knew a doctor around the corner in an apartment building-and gave my mother the apartment number. She told her that she could go right now because the doctor was there and would see me. My mother went even though she felt unsure, and as if in a trance rang the apartment number. A man answered and told her he was the doctor and to come right up. My mother described him as being dressed in white, with a gentle angelic face and a soft speaking voice. He told my mother that he could help with a treatment that could only be done twice….it was a radiation rock that he would tape over the mark on my face for just 4 seconds. My mother (within her altered consciousness) agreed. Then he said, "I can only do this one more time, then we will see what happens. Come back tomorrow." When my mom went to pay him he said, "Let us wait to see first." My mother came again the next day and he repeated the treatment, and he told my mother to come back in two weeks. At this point my mother cried and he placed his hand on her shoulder and said "she will be fine."

I was fine. The mark was gone in two weeks and my mother went back to pay the doctor. She rang the bell over and over again, and no one answered, so she rang the superintendent's bell. The super told my mother there was no doctor in that apartment or anywhere in the building and she said, "I was here two weeks ago and the doctor in that apartment healed my daughter." "Impossible," he said, "that apartment has been empty for the last 6 months!"

After all this time my mother still could not believe what happened and she was shaking and crying the whole time while telling me the story. She then showed me a photo of myself as a little baby with a mark as big as a silver dollar on my forehead. As I looked at the picture, I felt deep gratitude.

My first memory of my Guardian Angel was when I was six years old. At that time I experienced a great trauma, which was based in so much pain and confusion that I chose to block the experience for many years. Through my realizing how the

Creator had sent me ASTRA, my guardian angel to guide and protect me, the memory returned. -- My sister, who was eleven months older than I, pushed me in front of a moving car. I rolled to the curb and blacked out. A neighbor who was walking his dog saw what happened. He picked me up, carried me home, and told my mother what he had seen. My mother fell into deep denial. Even though she knew this man well, she rejected his words. I heard her saying, "No, No, that did not happen! I can't believe it!"

(Although I have now forgiven my 7 year old sister, this trauma created for me the lifelong challenge of constantly needing to confront my fears).

Fear of death consumed me and in days I became ill. While lying in my bed in the middle of the night with my head aching, I saw my room fill with brightly lit white, floating candles. I began to scream. My mother heard my cries and came running in and I yelled to her, "Mommy, don't touch the candles! Watch out! They will burn you!"

My mother cried, "Oh, my God, she's burning up!" For the rest of the night my parents worked together to break my fever. They put me in a tub of ice water and rubbed me down with alcohol. My fever broke on the following day and almost immediately thereafter, I began hearing what sounded like a male voice speaking in my head. I heard a soft and loving voice.

I had always been a frightened child, I was afraid of everything from the dark to snowflakes falling on my eyelashes, but most of all I was frightened of the spirits that often stood at the foot of my bed and floated around outside my window. I couldn't understand why they were there for they never spoke, and I would plead with my sister to tell them to go away.

When I was eight, my sister and I with two other girlfriends were playing indoors with our dolls. It was raining, when all of a sudden, I looked up, and standing at the glass front door was a beautiful little old man, carrying a crooked wooden cane. He was wearing a long white robe....his hair and his beard, were white. He had the most beautiful twinkling blue eyes that beckoned to me, and I wanted to go to him. Instead, I cried to my friends, "Look at that little old man there!"

My friends asked, "Where, Anna?"

"Over there" I cried! "Open the door and let him in."

"What man, Anna, Where?" My friends asked bewildered.

I just couldn't understand why they didn't see him, and when they ran to the door and opened it, the little old man had disappeared. I went outside and I was stunned as I looked up and down the street and he was nowhere in sight.

That night I told my father what happened and he believed my story. I was very relieved when he explained to me that perhaps it had been a grandfather from a past life who missed me very much. (My father was a believer in reincarnation) This made perfect sense to me.

From the time I began hearing The Voice, I didn't see ghosts anymore and thankfully, my fears diminished. The Voice continued to guide and encourage me not to be fearful.

The Voice would amuse me as well, by prompting me to announce things seconds before they would actually happen. For example, when members of my family were listening to the radio, The Voice would tell me to say the exact words that the radio announcer was about to say. After hearing this, my family was shocked, but they always attributed such phenomena to what they believed was my great imagination.

I still didn't understand why I could hear The Voice when no one else could. My sister, however, came to trust The Voice after an experience that we had one day while walking together. We had come upon a vacant lot where some books were lying on the ground. She wanted to take a closer look but The Voice warned me that a man was in there with a big stick. I told her what The Voice had said, but she didn't believe me and went into the vacant lot. Suddenly, a man came at her with a big stick. She screamed, and we turned and ran all the way home. From that day forward she would constantly ask me, "Anna what does The Voice say?"

When I was around eleven years old, my sister started telling our friends about The Voice and soon after that our friends told me that their parents said "Anyone who hears voices must be crazy." I was devastated. I began to worry that I might actually be crazy because I just couldn't understand why no one else ever heard The Voice. I became deeply saddened to think that this "Voice" from which I felt so much love and security, might not be real after all.

I was confused and lonely, and during this sad time in my life, I experienced an awakening so powerful that it remains with me today: One sunny summer afternoon, I was walking alone, when suddenly I was floating above the ground; my feet no longer touched the pavement and I felt myself expanding, I was everywhere all at once! I felt myself in the trees, the flowers, and the sky....indeed I was the trees, the flowers, and the sky! It was absolutely breathtaking, and so incredibly joyful. Then it was suddenly over. Once I felt my feet back on the pavement, I heard The Voice saying, "*Now it is time for you to walk through your fears, Anna, no one will help you.... you must do it yourself, but remember I am always with you. Even though you will not hear me for a while remember that I am with you and I would never leave you.*"

I didn't hear The Voice again for many years except in times of danger. One of these times was when I was a young married woman with two children. A friend was installing a new Formica counter top in my kitchen and as I leaned against my oven watching him spread the glue, I was startled to hear The Voice shouting in my head, "*Get your coat and go outside!*" Stunned, I instantly froze. The next thing I remember was feeling being pushed out the back door into the yard, (where my children were), by an invisible force.

I yelled to my friend to get out of the house, forgetting in that moment that he couldn't hear me because he was deaf. As soon as I stepped outside, I heard an explosion and the whole house became engulfed in flames. Thank God my friend had escaped serious injury, suffering only minor burns to his hands. The pilot light in the oven had ignited the fumes from the glue causing the explosion.

As we all stood outside watching my house turn into smoldering ash, I was struck by the realization that material things could be lost or destroyed in an instant. I knew then that I wanted something more in my life….this I had known for some time. Going through this catastrophe I was able to access this realization from a deeper and more profound place….from the depth of my being! I also realized another crucial fact: that I would have been killed were it not for the warning I received from The Voice, which I now recognized as my Guardian Angel.

The something more I had always wanted was to become an actress. So I joined an acting class in New York City, and for the first time in my life I felt as if I were following my true nature. Yet my road to self-discovery was not smoothly paved. I found myself in a tiny walk up apartment in New York City, and my family split-apart. I was divorced and at this time my teenage children began to pull away from me, blaming me for everything that we had lost. This created in me a great conflict, and I fell into self- doubt and deep despair.

One night while lying in bed with my fourteen year old daughter sleeping beside me, I was feeling so depressed that for the first time in my life I felt I really wanted to die. Then all of a sudden I saw a beautiful white light streaming diagonally across the closet door at the foot of my bed, and I watched in awe as it grew bigger and brighter until it expanded to the full length of the closet. As the light got brighter and whiter, I was overcome by the sensation of deep joy fluttering within my chest….this joy seemed to be separate from me however, as I felt it moving out of my chest going towards the light.

Words cannot describe my exhilaration when I realized that the feeling of joy was emanating from both the light and my desire to unite with the light. However, at the same time I also thought that my children needed me and I couldn't leave them. I looked over at my daughter who was sleeping beside me, and in that moment the white light dimmed and the joyous feeling (energy) subsided. I got out of bed and sat in the kitchen for the rest of the night. I was enraptured….I knew that God had given me a choice….to either return to Him or remain here. Knowing that I had made the choice to stay for my children (even though I had no means to support them), where was I supposed to go from here? What did God want me to do? How was I even to find out?

I searched for guidance and was led to a school in New York City where they taught practical philosophy and meditation. Having been blessed with a philosophical father, my mind and heart were open to all spiritual teachings which would speak to me.

It was there that I met Jeannie. She approached me one day after class and invited me for coffee. She explained that her husband had died six months earlier and that he had been communicating with her through automatic writing; now she was receiving messages for me and what was said was, "*Tell Anna that she has a very long wavelength of energy and that God wants her to connect to her Angel.*"

How was I to accomplish this? Through Jeannie's automatic writing, her husband answered me, "*Meditate Anna, meditate.*"

One day after deep meditation and prayer, while asking for God's guidance, I heard The Voice say, "*Anna pick up the pen,*" and as I did so a force moved my hand slowly across the paper.

The message read, "*Anna, hello, I am your Guardian Angel.*" My angel's first instruction for me was, "*Anna you must learn how to trust.*"

I had done it! I had made contact.

After three days of writing however, I was exhausted. When I finally asked why the energy was writing so slowly and why was I so tired, I was instructed to light a white candle and I did so. When I picked up the pen again, my hand flew across the page, and I wrote eight pages without stopping.

After working with automatic writing for six months, the Guardian Angel taught me much about myself and about the spiritual world of energy to which I am connected. At the Angel's request I also wrote for others; I was reluctant at first, but was reminded that all I had to do was to hold the pen and the Angel would speak through me. It wasn't long afterwards that I was given another incredible "gift" and even more reason to trust.

I had just climbed into bed preparing for sleep, and as soon as my head touched the pillow I heard a loud buzzing sound. Startled, I jumped up, and immediately the buzzing stopped. I put my head down again, and the buzzing returned, and I jumped up again, this time in great fear. I sat up for a while trying to understand what was happening. I decided that it was possible that the Guardian Angel was trying to communicate with me. This thought calmed my fears and I lay back down and the buzzing automatically returned. I asked, "Is it you, Guardian Angel?" When the buzzing sound intensified, it started to penetrate my whole body. Then I relaxed, trusting that it was the Angel. Yet, when I tried to move my limbs, I was paralyzed!

Suddenly I heard a sound like a drill, and felt a pressure at the top of my head. After a few seconds the drilling moved to the lower back of my head and then to the right side just above my ear. At each point I heard the loud sound of a drill, and felt deep pressure, but there was no physical pain. Finally the drilling stopped, and with my head still resting on the pillow and my eyes opened, I saw a shower of Mandalas coming at me like shooting stars. I watched in fascination at the most beautiful array of patterns and vivid colors that I had ever seen, for each Mandala was more beautiful and breathtaking than the one before it. This light show of energy continued for some time and then suddenly stopped. My body was then released from the paralysis. I sat up and wept at this experience and felt overwhelming joy....because I knew that I had been in God's presence.

I asked my Guardian Angel for an explanation of what had happened to me. *"Anna,"* was the reply, *"you have just witnessed your own energy, what you have seen are all the patterns, colors, and vibrations that you have created through all of your incarnations in both spirit and physical form. If you could see your True Essence, this is what you would see and hear, for you are, sound, you are patterns of color and vibration within the Light....and you have seen how magnificent you are in Truth."*

Soon after this experience my Guardian Angel told me that my channeling would take on a new form and in order for this to happen, I would have to cross and return over a great body of water. In doing so, I would receive the energy necessary to become the meditative channel that I am today. Since I had no plans to cross any ocean, and no money to do so, I was worried and kept asking, "How am I going to do that?" Always the answer came back, *"Anna, you must learn to trust."*

Approximately two months later, a young man from Norway, who was a member of my spiritual group in New York City, introduced me to his mother who had come to visit him. I agreed to channel for her through automatic writing, and she was so impressed that she invited me to come to Norway, where I would stay with her and make enough money to pay for my trip; again I was astounded at the power of my Guardian Angel.

When I returned home three weeks later, I sat down with a close friend to channel using the pen, and as I began to write, I heard, *"Anna, just listen."* I was still hesitant and continued to write. Suddenly the pen began writing faster and faster until it flew out of my hand and sailed across the room, and my friend burst out laughing. My friend said, "Anna, I think that you should just listen," so I did. As my body began rotating, I could feel the energy filling me, and a voice began to speak, the words just popped out of my mouth. At that point my friend asked the Angel, "Who are you? Do you have a name?" The Angel replied, *"I am God Energy....I am not a spirit, nor an entity, and if you prefer to call me by name than you may call me ASTRA."* (I found out later that `ASTRA` means star.) Through the wisdom of the Guardian Angel ASTRA, I have learned without question that we are all here to heal ourselves, for every Be-ING comes into physical body with the purpose of the soul, which is to heal the misguided perceptions of our false Ego personality in order for each of us to unite with whom we truly are, in Truth.

Along the path that ASTRA has led me I have learned of my own True identity....clearly I have seen God within my own Be-ING within all of Creation. Connecting to this wisdom required many years of passing through darkness and struggle....yet without those experiences I would never have been able to understand all that I AM. I have gained a deep peace within my heart that gently guides me through each day reminding me that whenever something negative occurs, I am not that negativity....I am instead, the Creative Force that is always unlimited in its movement and consequently, I can never be threatened by the illusions that take form in my physical world.

The Creative Force is within each of us....it is the seat of power that every person possesses because every person is an extension, a reflection of the `One`....and only through our own experiences and creativity, can we truly connect to our God-self.

My life has been dedicated to serving the Creator, and through my beautiful gift of ASTRA, my guardian angel, I have been guided to learn many lessons and to help many people with deep questions concerning their own purpose in this life. My belief is that you will also find the answers you are seeking within these teachings as well.

Love-in-Light, Anna Harlas

FOREWORD

We are very complicated humans, for we ourselves are not conscious enough to see the `Multi-Layers` of energy from which we are created and therefore, we become trapped by our lack of knowledge. `Know thyself!` This statement holds truth for once we realize what we do not know only then can we begin to understand anything. Here is the reason for writing this book: to assist us in learning who we are in truth, to recognize the energies that comprise us, the instincts that drive us, and to acknowledge the foundation of our existence. These teachings are here to enable us to clear away the debris of illusion which we have carried with us through.... many, many, incarnations of learning experiences. Through experiencing our creative connection to all of existence, we recognize our `true power` as the Creator, manifested in physical form, embedded within the dense energy, of the Ego, (i.e., the Earth Plane).

This book speaks about God; hopefully, you will understand that `God` is a word which describes the Force of Energy... .a central pulse from which all creation flows. Any word that you believe implies, the central pulse of the Creative Force, can be substituted for the word `God.` I use `God` because I am comfortable with the power that vibrates from this word-and I have great reverence for the Energy it ignites in me. <u>We are God! We are this Center, but we do not remember this Truth.</u> ASTRA guides my consciousness to awaken the memory of this Truth; this book was written to ultimately guide your consciousness to this awakening as well.

The book is divided into categories. It begins by describing the levels of energy which compose our physical existence as human beings. It then goes on to examine each level of energy; by illuminating the qualities we possess within our True Nature such as love, trust, acceptance, and courage, to name a few. There is a natural movement that guides us into opening our Third Eye, creating for each of us a new direction of thought process, which is more direct, and truthful, then the direction in which we now experience our thoughts.

You will see words such as `Ego Body,` God-self,` `Creator,` `God mind,` `Ego mind,` `God-consciousness,` `Ego-consciousness,` `Child-self,` `Inner-world` and `Be- ING,` also the word `energy` will be used frequently throughout the book. The reason for this is that right from the beginning you will understand that we are all energy. How we perceive this energy is what creates our world, and ultimately our personal selves. The word `perception,` is used frequently throughout the book as well. The word `Mani- fester,` is used to describe our ability to create our own life within God's image. All of these terms will be clearly understood, for they will be explained within the context of that which is being described. They will be repeated frequently, to enable you to follow easily, the train of thought that is guiding these teachings.

I will be using experiences from my group work, in order to demonstrate in a very simple, practical, and functional manner how the teachings apply to each of us. I will present the Angel's words as they have come to me in meditation. I will offer clarification in my own words, where necessary to further your understanding of what is being said.

There will be questions by members of my group, followed by answers from ASTRA. My thoughts will follow each ingredient.... in Chapter IX, `The Nine Ingredients-With-in Your True Nature.`

Many words are capitalized, such as `truth,` `love,` `whole,` and `one` when the meaning of each is interchangeable with the word `God.` The word `Be-ING` is capitalized because it encompasses both the male and female, human being.

The Guardian Angel speaks in its own cosmic language, periodically using past, present, and future tenses, in accordance with that language. I have not edited this usage, in order to maintain the natural rhythm and flow. Also you will notice the use of the masculine gender pronouns `he`- `his` and `him` throughout the book. This reflects the true essence of the Ego, which is masculine in nature, even though all humans are made up of both masculine and feminine energy....it is the Ego that dominates the consciousness of both sexes in earthly life.

You will see that the words of the Guardian Angel are printed for easy identification with a star symbol to show that `ASTRA` is speaking. This will aid the reader to focus into the rhythm of the Guardian Angel, thereby, connecting the reader to the `Multi-Layers` that comprise the wisdom of `ASTRA.`

In Chapter XI `ASTRA's Personal Guidance,` the reader is experiencing spontaneous conversations with the group. This is not edited to read as the body of the book reads. I added these channels for the purpose of presenting a personal connection with ASTRA, (the angelic guide), creating the experience of being part of the group.

Now the time has come for you to begin your relationship with the Guardian Angel `ASTRA.` I can only trust with deep love in my heart for all of creation that you will read on and receive the Light of your own love, which will free you, as it continues to free me, from the `darkness` that we as Sleeping Be-ings Create.

Be blessed on your journey,
Love-in-Light,
Anna

CHAPTER I
THE FALL OF MAN THROUGH EGO

ASTRA Speaks...

*I will explain Ego and its beginning. The Ego is within everything that you do, that you think. Ego is a manifestation of illusion....it is the illusion that separates Man from God. When you are within mind, you are within Ego. Within your Be-ING the Ego-mind separates you from the mind of God. I now speak to you of the Ego-mind, the mind that thinks within the human body. This is Ego! It controls all the thought processes and it is in total denial of your God-mind. **Your Ego separates you from God.**

When man came into being at the beginning of human manifestation, the God-mind was present and man did not think in the way that he now does....he allowed God to speak through him. The process was a hearing as it is now, but man did not hear his Ego....he heard the God energy that created him. He functioned in harmony with nature and the rest of Creation, for God energy manifested in all shapes and substances, and all was in harmony until man began to get caught up in his `physical-ness.`

Experiencing the senses brought a very sharp and profound feeling of being, and man began to play with this experience by creating more and more manifestations to physically sense. In his development, an attachment to the physical body took place; once God/Man became attached to his senses within his physical body he disconnected from his God-mind....for he began to create a new mind (Ego), a mind that confirmed his illusions and made them his reality for he believed so strongly in the substances he experienced through his senses.

Believing in the material created even further separation from his God-mind, for now man became absorbed in his feelings and emotions. He began to weave the web of illusion still further by trapping himself through the senses. He began to feel confusion for his physical manifestations were coming too quickly into being and there was no (True understanding) of their purpose....for there was no longer a Higher Guidance directing his creating. Man created beyond his own understanding and found himself using the Ego-mind more and more in order to find reason for his emotions and his desires. Ego-mind became stronger and stronger in controlling the power on the Earth Plane, for now the God power was being <u>disguised</u> by the Ego and man quickly lost memory of his true self.

Without memory of the `Self,` man is like a child lost in the wilderness looking for his father and trying to survive without him. Man began to rely more and more on what he calls the `power of reason` which, in truth, was man's attempt to create a foundation on which he could simplify or eliminate his confusion. As frightened children react when they are feeling threatened, mankind reacts through the Ego with judgment, criticism, and fear.

Through the remnants of memory that continue to live on the Earth Plane in nature, man still can attach to that link which can bring him into his memory of Truth. Nature is not affected by this manifested Ego because it accepts the God energy without a thinking mechanism to block it, but man's ability to connect to the laws of nature through his thinking mechanism allows him to save himself from this great darkness and loss.... so he may recognize himself from without in order to create the journey from within to the perfect union of Oneness that is known through his God-mind.

We will now speak of the practical road to follow in regaining your memory of your God-self. The practical road to take in opening the memory that connects you to your God-mind exists in what is available in your present reality....what is available is the Ego, and therefore, the road back is through the Ego-mind. You need to use the tools that have been created out of your Highest-vibration. The powers of reason and discrimination are valuable for these are the highest vibrations that are perceived through the Ego-mind....and you must make use of them on your journey to your God-self. You do this in multitudes of ways. It takes work because you are not yet able to recognize all the negative perceptions of your Ego-you are dealing yet with Karma that was created out of Ego experiences.

In order to bring the particular Karma into its balancing and releasing of the Ego's negative perceptions, you must open to your God-mind where you can see beyond the surface of what has taken place and learn the lesson that the event holds for awakening your memory of who you are, in Truth. All perception through Ego is negative-all Karma holds negativity; even what you may call a 'good' Karma is Ego-originated. Your God- mind possesses no Karma. It is free to create and cannot be captured by the physical, the material. It is not confined to the body, for it is all that exists within the moment.

Karma is blocked energy, blocked in fear and confusion through the Ego's attachment to the physical body. It is a creation of limitation rather than freedom, in that the Ego becomes captured by the experience. The reasoning part of the mind tells you that anything that creates unhappiness, discomfort and pain (physically or mentally) is negative, and you try to avoid these feelings as much as is humanly possible; but the reasoning mind also tells you they seem not to be avoidable, that you fall into patterns of thinking and behavior that create this negativity through what seems no fault of your own. You must stop to remember that there is no such thing as fault-only reality….and the reality clearly states that you are the creator of your own circumstances.

The Ego, out of fear, wants to control everything around the individual-thinking mechanism, and it fantasizes constantly, taking reality and embellishing it with fictitious ideas in an attempt to remain in power over circumstances that are confusing to it. The confusion is coming from Karma, for the Ego has yet no memory of the past experiences; and in spite of no memory, action arises over and over again that creates discomfort….and the Ego attempts to alter the discomfort through manipulation- sometimes it ignores feelings and emotions and sometimes it creates repeated behavior from the past, unconscious of what is taking place in the moment. This unconsciousness creates more Karma and keeps the Ego-mind continually fighting for an identity.

This is now clear: That in order to reach the God-mind, you must overcome past Karma by creating balance in your energy and bringing the past into your consciousness to view the lessons once more and come to a clear understanding of them with your whole Be-ING.

You need to make some very important changes in your perception of life. You need to see some vitally powerful truths: one, that you are the Creator and you are totally responsible for what you think, what you understand, and, especially, what you feel and what you create from within and manifest from without. You need to see your own power....you are capable of flowing into a consciousness that provides happiness, love, and peace.

Your spirit needs to flow into certain religious ideas within the Spiritual Light, such as the Devil and God....seeing that the Devil, in truth, is your negativity (Ego), and God is your Positive Energy (Love). When you hear `thou shall have no other God before me,` understand the meaning to be that you will hold the Power and Light of God within and you will not give it over to another person, idea, or material thing....you will stand composed within the Light, following its guidance as the captain follows the light in the sky to pilot his sailing ship. You are the captain, God is the Light, your Ego is the ship- the ship, alone, trying to control its destination, will run aground. Because the Ego fears, it needs to control....your God-self has no desire to control, for within your God-self you trust the Light to guide you through all the storms and calm seas, as well….your God- self has no fear!

To transform the Ego-mind you need to be conscious of how your Ego thinks, and then you can gain the wisdom to guide and teach through love and patience the frightened Ego (child). These are virtues that you consciously know about, but the Ego does not allow you to experience them too often. You must put them into action in order to gain balance in your mind, for at this time you are divided in your Mental Body- you are of two minds (the God-mind and the Ego-mind); this division creates the pain and decay on the Earth Plane. You need to align your Ego-mind to your God-mind.

Balancing Karma and letting go of the Ego's desire to control and manipulate through fear is the goal. That is why I say to you this is work, for you need a very important element here in order to do this work-you need to trust and have blind faith in the positive and loving side of your own nature, which is God. It takes a brave soul to cast aside that which is familiar (that which has been constant throughout many lifetimes) in the hope and belief that there is something much higher at hand. Very few souls are at the level in their development where they can release and let go all at once….it is a gradual process….it can only be done through concentration and focus in a short span of your time--**in the moment.**

You must learn to become conscious of every moment as if it were all that existed because, in truth, it is all that exists. This is a very important step in letting go of Ego control in your life, for by focusing in the moment (into the reality of what exists there) you cannot bring in anything from the past or create fantasy of the future, which is the habit of your Ego. In a true sense, this focusing in the reality of the moment leaves you exposed and vulnerable. This is good, for that vulnerability is what allows the God-mind to manifest.

Make a mental picture….see yourself as you are, in truth, at this moment: two minds, the God-mind and the Ego-mind. See that your Ego-mind is now in control and has lost connection to the God-self through fear; yet the God-mind of your Be-ING stands waiting to be revealed in your life and only the love that you hold for yourself will create its manifestation.

Transforming your Ego is the next step in human development, for the Ego has become a negative force in humanity. Your Ego interferes with your Emotional Body, which is the thread that connects Spirit to all of your Bodies* this thread is becoming frayed and weak and the energy that is passing through it from Spirit to Body is missing its mark.

In order to save mankind, the Ego is to be transformed into pure God energy and become a source of new creativity for man and woman on the Earth Plane, for through the Ego you view everything in reverse of truth; a new and truthful perception must be acquired through the Ego. By creating a new strength at your center (the <u>Heart)</u> you can carry yourself through the process of letting go of old ideas and beliefs, leaving you an empty vessel waiting to be filled with the Spirit of God. On this journey you are loved and guided through the memory of self.

---

* "Bodies" will be explained in detail in Chapter II.

CHAPTER II
SEVEN BODIES OF ENERGY

ASTRA Speaks....

*You are told that you are not your body. What this means is that you are not just the body - YOU ARE ENERGY. You cannot deny that you have a body and that the body is very important. After all, everything you feel comes through the senses off the Physical Body, everything you see comes through the physical eyes of the body, and all sensation, joyful and painful, is experienced through the Physical Body. What naturally takes place is that your Egos become very attached to the Physical Body, believing that the body is substantial and, therefore, is who you are. In truth, it is only part of who you are, for you are Seven Bodies of Energy; and until you become conscious of this truth you will be eternally trapped within the illusion of the Physical Plane....for when you operate from this belief you have a limited view of the world, you see only part of the creation, a very small part, a part that is obsessed with the material (solidly formed matter) and the Physical Body.

`You cannot see beyond your nose,` as you would say. In truth, the Physical Body is the lowest in position, for it is the closest to the gross matter, the density of the Earth Plane. In your obsession with it you pull all of your other Bodies down into the gravity fields of the Earth, causing them to be overshadowed by the material form, rendering them powerless, and sentencing yourselves to the Ego Body, the creator of fear, judgment, separation, and pain, equaling decay. This is why you feel powerless because you have given your power away through your attachment to the Physical Body.

In Truth the physical body is energy, `energy` is a word that is not clearly understood by most physical Be-ings, for they believe energy is invisible and moves quickly through the air and is captured by man and channeled through a physical object in order to ignite power, such as electricity in the Physical Plane. This perception separates man from clearly understanding energy in its true form, for energy is visible as well as invisible. Energy moves quickly or does not move at all. It is seen through everything that exists, for everything is Energy. You, as Physical Be-ings, are energy. There are parts of your energy that you see as the Physical Body and there are parts that are unseen.

We shall, at this time, describe the Bodies of your Energy. We shall use the word `body` because you are attached to this Physical Body of energy and you will understand more clearly through picturing a body of energy. You are, in truth, Seven Bodies of Energy. At the gross level you are *1: the Physical Body, then rising into your Heavenly bodies you are *2: the Ether Body, *3: the Astral Body, *4: the Emotional Body, *5: the Mental Body, *6: the Ego Body, *7: the Spiritual Body.

The energy of the Mental Body moves quickly, for thoughts move quickly. The energy that is trapped in the Physical

Body is contained in a structure and does not move on its own, so, therefore, it can become stagnant energy. That is why decay manifests in the physical form and the body dies. You are energy connected to the Whole of existence through the Spiritual Body. The Emotional Body connects the vastness of your Be-ING through the Spiritual Body to the dense Physical Body, for it is through the Emotional Body that you experience all of your Energy. Therefore, the Emotional Body is your teacher and awakens you to all of your energy. The Ether Body ignites the physical, breathes life into the dense energy, and assists in creating movement of energy within the confinements of the Physical Plane. The Astral Body works through the dream state to awaken your whole Be-ING to recall your True Identity.

What remains now is the Ego Body. The following material will focus strongly on this body, for it is the body that divides your consciousness, that blocks out the Energy existing beyond the Physical Body. It is the `illusionary/perception` of the Ego Body that every human being holds within the cells, the atoms, the electrons of his structure.

Everything is of one Energy, for everything is `One,` in Truth....so all that exists is existing through the Creator God. What this means is that all things are connected. As within your own body, one organ is connected to the other, as the veins of your body flow through your whole system connecting the nervous system to the organs. Through the Mental Body (Mind of God) everything is operating as one unit, so the whole of Creation is operating as one unit, for all is connecting. Visualize through your perception the whole of the universe as one body and understand that you are part of that One. In order for you to see this more clearly, we are breaking down the levels of energy so they can be clear for your Ego-consciousness to understand. We are breaking your body down to seven levels of energy in order for you to see that you are, as a Whole Be-ING, a part of a greater Whole.

To recognize the Greater Whole, you must first recognize how you are structured in your pattern of energy; so visualize your Physical Body and see an aura of **red** energy coming off very close to the Physical Body, shining off of the physical, as if you were outlining your Physical Body with a red crayon. This energy you can see, for it is manifested in the physical form. Continue to look and see an inch away from the red line, the energy of the Ether Body; see this as an **orange** color and have yourself, outlined in this vibration. Now go an inch beyond that line, and see the energy of your Astral Body being drawn in a **yellow** color. Go yet an inch beyond the yellow and see the energy of the Emotional Body in a color **green**. Go an inch beyond the green and see the color of the Mental Body come through in **deep blue**. Now we are going to see beyond to the color of the Ego Body which is **purple**. Then we are going to draw in the Spiritual Body, which goes beyond, in **white**. As you see the colors of your energy coming off of your physical structure you are recognizing the spectrum, as you know it, of color, for you are the spectrum of color....you are the spectrum of the Whole.

For your further visual understanding, we will connect the colors of your energy to the physical centers, which are called `Chakra,` within your body, connecting, first, the **red** color of your Physical Body to your root Chakra which is located in the lower part of your body near your reproductive organs. We will connect the **orange** color of the Ether Body to the Chakra of the Ether Body located at the navel of your Physical Body. We will connect the **yellow** color of the Astral Body to the Astral Chakra, which is the solar plexus that you find in the area of the stomach in the Physical Body. We will connect the **green** color of the Emotional Body to the heart Chakra of the body, at the center of the chest. We will connect the **deep blue** color of the Mental Body to the Mental Body Chakra in the throat. We will connect the **purple** color of the Ego Body to the Ego Body Chakra in the third eye, the lower forehead between the physical eyes. We will connect the color **white** of the Spiritual Body to the Chakra in the crown of the head.

Now you have a picture of your energy, seeing the energy take form in color and seeing the energy housed within your Physical Body at the Chakra to which it is connected, for you are to begin to see more and more the connection between all things….by learning the connection of your energy to your physical structure.

CHAPTER III
THE SEVEN BODIES OF ENERGY THAT CREATE YOUR WHOLENESS

I directed my class to ask about each individual body, and the participants did so in their questions to ASTRA. I am guided to share with you the information received in regard to each body; and at the end of the description of a particular body I will add questions and answers that will also, I believe, assist you in learning more about yourself as energy.

1. THE PHYSICAL BODY

ASTRA Speaks:

*We are to speak of the word `human` to be human, the human condition, the gross matter, the physical Be-ING, `physicalness` of your Be-ING. You are very complicated Be-ings and there are many levels to you. Even as you are manifested as a human on the Physical Plane, you have many other bodies of energy with you, not only the Physical Body. You are always aware of the Physical Body but you are not always conscious of your other bodies of energy.

We will discuss what it is to be a human in a Physical Body.

Does this mean to be only a flesh and blood creature? No. To be human is to be one with all of your bodies, to be connected to your Wholeness, but we shall now separate the bodies, isolate them, in order to clarify their function within the Whole.

Beginning here, with the Physical Body, when it is isolated it becomes clear that it is of the animal kingdom, that it survives through its instinctual nature....so we are isolating parts of your energy that create your whole Be-ING, as you would isolate a part of the energy in a single cell in order to diagnose a disease within that structure.

As a physical Be-ING, the goal is survival. At the base level, it is expressed through the physical form. When you are hungry, you eat; when you are tired, you sleep; when you are threatened, you fight. That which takes place through the physical form is an automatic response to what is coming at you from without. You are programmed to respond to what manifests in order to secure your survival in the dense, gross matter of the Earth Plane.

Thinking of yourself in this way, begin to see how your needs are met for physical continuation. The human body is built to withstand changes in temperature and it responds to the cold by drawing in to concentrate on its inside mechanism that generates heat. It also is built to be able to eat a great variety of foods, such as plant life, animal life, and insects, so the human body does not easily starve in the Physical Plane. The human being is a social creature for the continuation of his species. He is drawn to sexual activity in order to reproduce. He instinctively becomes part of a tribe in order to survive invasion from other species, so he is, through his instincts, drawn to a family structure that builds a shield, a wall of protection, around his Physical Body. When you look at that part of your Be-ING as in isolation, you begin to see more and more how you are connected to the animal kingdom, to nature itself.

You are on the chain of survival; you are at the top of the chain only because you have incorporated your other bodies into your physical structure, for what makes you most unique are the unseen Chakra within your Physical Body that house the energy of your other bodies, creating your Wholeness. No other species is equipped to house other bodies and integrate them throughout the physical form. Only the human is blessed with this gift which puts you at the top of the chain of survival.

You may ask your questions now on the Physical Body, on what it is to be human within the Earth Plane. You may begin.

Q. To me the word `human` has always been something a little different than the Physical Body. It's always been a way of behaving or acting while you are here, a way of being merciful, loving, or compassionate.

This is good, for, in truth, to be human is to be God-manifested on the Earth Plane, for you are in this plane as the God Energy, to behave as the God Energy, to create through the God Energy which is all balanced energy....love and compassion, balance and perfection. But all souls are not aware of this truth. You are aware on one level only, but on many other levels there are other interpretations that you live by when you hear the word `human.` You live through the Ego which believes the human to be superior to all things, to be the master, the dictator, the selfish energy that creates to enhance its own power, its own grand idea of itself. On some level in every human there is this desire, and there is this type of manifestation somewhere in even the most balanced energy. But it is important that you learn `from the bottom up,` as you may say. Let us talk more about the human and how the human behaves in its environment. Speak of your humanness. What is it about yourself that you do, think, or act that tells you, you are human?

Q. To me, I guess it means that we are multifaceted, that we have many levels to operate on both spiritually and physically.

Yes, those are the bodies of which we have spoken, but we are not going to work with those other bodies at this time. We are only to speak of the human body, that which is the physical matter which is within the gross plane the physical flesh and blood body. Focus on it alone and see how you operate on this gross level. Do not bring in your other bodies, though they are present; at this point isolate the physical and discover that which is of the gross vibration within your Physical Being.

Q. I guess I would say it's like a living physical matter, like a plant that we keep alive and nourish.

A plant, something that you give to….the plant starts out as a seed and you continuously feed it so it may grow. The plant has no thought pattern; it does not see anything beyond its own need for nurturing; and it is isolated as it sits within the earth, as it shoots off its growth, its foundation, its roots to travel and seek out for itself what it needs to survive. Man does this the human does this. He is built to survive and he instinctively gives to himself in order to accomplish this. At this level there is no thinking, for when he is operating on his instincts he feels and he is pulled by his feelings. When the Body is cold, for instance, it reacts to the cold and it pulls itself in so it may become warmer, generating its inner heat. We are speaking here of the instincts. As the animal kingdom has its instincts and the plant kingdom has its instincts so does man, the physical Being have his instincts. Man's instincts are altered through his perception, through all his other bodies; yet when you strip away to the physical Body alone, you can see how much man is one with the other kingdoms of nature. There is no difference between them. Man melds into the Oneness.

Q. I think that being human means being able to experience and make mistakes and to not be as perfect as your spiritual self would be. In other words, it's your chance to learn, `to go to school` here.

This is the plane in which you learn many lessons. This is the plane in which you work to balance your karma; yet when we speak of these things, we speak of the other bodies. We speak of the Emotional Body; we speak of the Spiritual Body. Try to speak of the gross body alone. It is difficult to separate, isn't it? It is difficult to separate all the other bodies from the flesh and blood body because all the other bodies are part of it. It is all one; yet we are seeking to strip the other bodies away so we may see how connected to the earth the Physical Body is, in truth.

Try to visualize yourself as just the body, just the body that works on instinct alone, which has its needs and wants from its cellular structure; and these needs and wants, are provided for because that is what keeps the body alive and functioning.

Let us look at the body on that level. It may not be easy, so use your imagination, if you have to think of your body as not being able to speak, that would be good. This way it has no vocabulary, no thinking mechanism. It's just a body, nothing more. Let us not think that this body has anything more than instincts; only flesh and blood. Now thinking of it in this way, what are the needs of this body?

Q. Is sex a need of the Physical Body?

Yes, it is a need, for only then can it reproduce. In order for the species to survive it needs to reproduce; therefore, it must have sexual activity, as all animal and plant life have sexual contact in order to reproduce. This is a need, a function of the body, and it is there for the body's survival alone. Do not think of the other levels of sexual activity that you have learned through your other Bodies, meaning the emotional connection to sexual intercourse that comes from the emotional experience through the love energy. Focus on the gross matter. In this matter it is function and instinct only. Something happens to the chemistry of the body to create an attraction which pulls the body to another life form and there it instinctively acts on a feeling which creates a sexual union and a new life. There is no emotion here only a need that creates an action.

Q. Because the body controls that which it needs, to keep itself alive, if you were to hold your breath and block your breathing, would you pass out before dying and would your body again take over the breathing?

This is correct. It is an instinct. Breathing is a function that exists without effort, for within this Plane there is air and gravity, and in order to survive, air must be taken inward. If you cut it off, the body will die. Before the body dies, it will fight to recapture the air. If it has to kill that which is blocking its air, it shall do so, for the instinct to have air is great, greater than the concern of life from without. The concern for life is always from within; it is at the center of every Be-ING; it is not from without! That is why you will always save yourself before you save another. Your instinct would be to preserve your own Be-ING. We are not speaking at the level of consciousness which would bring in a decision to save someone else; we are speaking of instinct for survival, which is at your center.

Q. I believe the human condition to be a domesticated primate. To live in community to have other primates to need a leader, and that there must be a long rearing between mother and child, a bonding. I see us as a domesticated variety.

This is correct. The human is a specific species and it needs to have connection with other humans, a family. Many of the other species have this in common, the need for a leader, the need to follow in the direction of the strongest Physical Be-ING.... for within the instinctual nature of the Physical Body the most powerful is always the strongest and ultimately becomes the leader, for it is the Be-ING who acts powerfully in a fearless way who leads the rest of the group. This is so in the animal kingdom, as well, and man is part of this kingdom.... man always follows the footsteps of the strongest link in his evolutionary chain. The instinct of the female to protect her young is also necessary for survival. A child left on its own would immediately run into obstacles that would destroy it, so there is a built-in instinct to nurture the young, which all of the animal kingdom possesses. This comes from the greed to survive. I use the word `greed` because within the physical (within the gross matter) it is a taking, it is whoever is the most fit, the most courageous, who survives best, who continues. Because of the deep desire to continue in all species within this plane, this instinct is built into the cellular level of your body.

There is no memory of your God-Self here, not at this level. At this level there is only a desire to survive. It is important that you see this clearly. It will help you to begin to understand your connection to this plane, to yourselves as creatures. You are creatures of the earth, and you have forgotten how deeply connected you are to this truth.

Q. Do you mean that we have forgotten because we recognize our spirituality?

You have forgotten because of the Ego that has distorted this truth. The Spiritual Body has knowledge of this union. It is the Ego working through the other bodies that distorts this truth. That is why you must see how complex you are, how many levels there are to your Be-ING, how much you must work through each level, what you must reconnect to and what you must release and let go of in order for you to become Whole. You must have all your bodies in perfect balance. This is why we are breaking down the bodies....in order for you to see their true function within the Whole, so you may understand more clearly what creates thought, emotion, desire, need, and so forth. As a puzzle we shall put everything together, fit one body into the next. You shall begin to see very clearly how you have gotten confused and disconnected from your other bodies. This insight shall bring you to a very high plane of consciousness.

2. THE ETHER BODY

We spoke about the Ether Body next. This body doesn't seem to be of this plane, and so we don't think about it very often. We can relate to having an Emotional Body and a Mental Body because we can visualize the connection to our Physical Body of heart and mind because the heart and brain are organs within the body. The Ether Body, however, is transparent, so we have trouble connecting to the idea that we are also this body. Here is what ASTRA told us about our Ether Body:

ASTRA Speaks….

*Everything has an Ether Body; the planet, itself, possesses an Ether Body, this body is the air that you inhale….and the space around you (it is that which ignites everything). All sound and vibration travel in the Ether Body. The Ether Body ignites the senses of your Physical Body. You cannot hear or taste without it, smell or feel objects. All sense of feeling travels in the Ether Body. This body is a moving energy and it breathes life into the illusion of the Earth Plane.

Reality manifests when elements of God Energy come together and ignite with this body. An example: if a Be-ING is deaf, there is a blockage in the Physical Body that prevents him from picking up the vibrations of the Ether Body. The Ether Body, itself, cannot be damaged for it is of the Ethereal Plane, a Heavenly Body; but it can be blocked through the Physical Body or plane. The Physical Body is energy, as all is energy; and when this energy becomes blocked on the Physical Plane the Ether Body is cut off at the point where it is blocked within the Physical Body, creating the manifestation of deafness, as an example. Energy must constantly move in order for life to exist, for movement creates more energy, more life. When energy is blocked there is no movement and the creation of new energy at that point is damaged; therefore, decay occurs. Blocked energy creates disease, a malfunction, within the physical Body.

How is energy blocked? It is blocked through the Mental Body and the Emotional Body, and, especially, through the Ego Body, for the Ego Body creates fear and fear is the most powerful block to life. Through these Bodies, you hold onto energy, and as you hold energy you block life. An example of this is, if you are emotionally upset and fearful of illness through your Ego Body, you obsess through the Ego and Emotional bodies; in this obsessing you block your energy and the flow of life is cut off at this point and you may become ill. The concern for the Physical Body creates a block of energy which then begins to decay in the Physical Body at the focus of the obsession, and the obsession is manifested into your reality. This blockage of energy takes many forms and is directed through every part of your existence. It can be the reason why relationships are blocked in their growth, or why they are not formed to begin with. It can manifest in disease of the Mental Body as well as the Physical Body; therefore, it is important to understand that when a Be-ING is born with a physical defect, this energy has a deep-routed block carried from past lifetimes into this life. That is why the defect is immediately manifested.

The Ether Body ignites all of your other bodies, and when you pass from this plane, the Ether Body is one of the first bodies to leave the physical. That is why there is no physical pain at the moment of death, because your Ether Body draws away, to allow the passing to take place.

The Ether Body supports the life of the physical. You must remember that the Physical Body and all of the physical things that you see on the Earth Plane are illusion. They are created from mind (your Mental Body) but they do not come to life until the Ether Body ignites them. The gross manifestations of the Earth Plane are ideas formed into matter. Until your six Heavenly bodies enter into the Physical Body, there is no life, no movement. That is why we call the second through the seventh bodies your Heavenly Bodies. Only the Physical Body (the first body) can decay, for only illusion can disappear.... and the Physical Body is illusion. Your other bodies are constant and they can enter and do enter into many other forms within creation....so your Physical Body is an ignited illusion, ignited by God.

Q. How do the Ether and Physical Bodies separate from each other? Are they separate from each other all of the time or can you explain that distinction?

The Ether Body separates at the point of the physical (death). There is an Ether Body within the planet itself, which keeps the life of the planet, the heart- beat, the spark ignited within the planet, within plant and animal life, within the waters. That Ether Body is always within a living organism. Your Ether Body goes back into the earth, into the plane, itself, after your use for it in the Physical Body has ceased. You drop this Body when you leave the Earth Plane. Your energy goes to other realms and other planes of consciousness and you are pure Spiritual Body; yet your Ether Body remains within the Earth Plane, flowing into other living organisms within the plane.

There are spirits trapped within the Physical Plane because the Ether Body does not completely separate from the Physical Body at death. This takes place when the death is premature, meaning accidental or by murder, and by energies that are obsessed through their Ego Bodies with the Physical Plane, itself. As in all things, death needs to be accepted by your whole Be-ING in order for your passing to the next level of consciousness to take place. If there is a block in your energy, a strong resistance to letting go, you will be separated from spirit and trapped in the Earth Plane until you are freed by a high and powerful spiritual entity (messenger, from God).

Q. Is all physical matter, as we understand it, backed by the Ether Body then, like the sun, and the other star planets and all physical things?

Yes, the Ether Body ignites (breathes life into) all physical things. Now we see the Physical Body more clearly. The Body is a shell, in truth, an illusion. It is created out of mind, out of the Mind of God. It is created by the Creator, and when it is ignited by the Ether Body it comes to life and the Creator is manifesting through it. See yourself, for example, as a sculptor molding a figure out of clay, creating an image in your mind, and see that you are the creator manifesting that image-that you are a vessel filling with God's will and moving through the dense energy of the Earth Plane, through the connection of the spirit to the One Mind. You are an animation drawn by God, ignited by the Ether Body, which is the breath of God. See yourself clearly at your beginning, an illusion created out of Mind, ignited by the Ether Body; and as we focus on the Ether Body, we focus on life, on breath, on movement. When the other bodies come into play, we will see how much the Ego manipulates your energy and how it has created separation from God (Truth).

Q. How will it help us to know that we are composed of seven bodies?

It is important for you to know the Self, how you are put together through the Mind of God, in order to be a perfect reflection of the One Energy and to experience the peace, joy and harmony that you are within this Truth.

Q. Is it the Ether Body that unites all people, all souls, or is it on a higher level that we are all connected into one organism, as is the planet?

The Ether Body's function is to breathe life into the illusion. It awakens the senses. It is part of the One but you are not connected to the Whole through the Ether Body or through any one of your bodies. You are connected to the Whole because you <u>are</u> the Whole. You are God-Manifested into the physical form, into the dense matter of the Earth Plane. Your lack of memory is what creates the need to work within the illusion, putting the pieces of yourself back together, as you would put a puzzle together, in order to see, to view the Whole and to reignite the memory of who you are, in Truth.

Q. What happens when the Physical Body is sleeping? Is it blocking off parts of the Ether Body so it doesn't hear or feel in order to sleep?

What is taking place here is that the Astral Body separates from your energy and is focused within the Astral Plane when you are within sleep, so all of your bodies, except for the Physical, are in focus in the Astral Body in this state. The Ether Body remains with you always when you are a living organism, but it is not in focus in the same way when you are sleeping, for all of your organs are slowed down in order for the focus to shift into Astral Plane. If the Ether Body were to leave, your organs would stop working and the body would die. You are being suspended between planes when you are within sleep. You are not grounded in the Earth Plane nor are you completely within the Astral Plane. All of your bodies go into the Astral Plane except for the Physical and Ego bodies. The physical is `hypnotized` (for want of a better description). It is drugged so it has no movement. All of this is taking place through the power of Spirit, for when you go to sleep your Spiritual Body is orchestrating all of the lessons and information that you are needing in order to bring the missing pieces together in your consciousness that will free you from illusion created by your Ego Body.

3. The Astral Body

By this time everyone in the Group, including myself, felt confusion about the concept of bodies and how we are made up of seven bodies of energy. The difficulty was in trying to imagine the separate function of each body and how each function could serve us in our physical lives; yet something compelled us to open and listen to what was being given, and we began to recognize more and more how we are served by acknowledging the energy that we are rather than the physical, material body that we believe we are.

As we approached the Astral Body, we began to see more clearly that we are not alone in this universe, that even within our own Physical Body we are not alone….that a Higher Intelligence lives within us and is working to guide us into a conscious state. We began to see this more clearly as ASTRA spoke to us about our Astral Body. I ask you now to open yourself to the information on the Astral Body that came next.

ASTRA Speaks….

*We are now to speak of the Astral Body. This is your Third Body as we place them in order, for all of them surface the Physical Body at a specific Chakra within it. The Body closest to the earth is the Physical Body; and each body that follows goes higher and higher off of the Physical Plane until you reach the Spiritual Body which is your highest body and is your direct connection to the God Plane. The Astral Body is in third position and is in the Chakra of the Solar Plexus within the Physical Body. You cannot see the form of your Astral Body in conscious state although it has form within the Astral Plane. It is a duplicate of the Physical Body that you see on the Earth Plane, the difference being that it is a body of light (transparent and weightless) and it moves to serve the Whole of your Be-ING by experiencing, testing, and reliving information that is needed to direct you in your healing.

There are physical Be-ings on the Earth Plane who are able to see the form within a conscious state because they are able to go into the Astral Plane and connect through the Mental Body to what is taking place. These Be-ings experience the weightlessness, the joy, the power of the Astral Plane. Those who are completely aligned with the power of this energy can many times manifest the Astral Body into dense form in order to be seen by other physical Be-ings. This is rare because most Be-ings on the Earth Plane are not able to experience themselves as the energy they are, in truth. Very few have the faith, the love, and the courage at this time in their evolution to experience the Astral Body in wakeful consciousness; when they go into Astral projection it is usually triggered by the body without the conscious knowledge of the Be-ING, and, therefore, there are Be-ings who work consciously to reproduce this state through manipulation of the body in order to experience the weightlessness and serenity, not recognizing its True Function.

The Astral Body's True Function is to serve through dream state, for in this state the Ego is not in control of your energies. The Spiritual Body is in control in this state. Why is this so? It is so because the Astral Body's function is to experience first in the Astral Plane that which will manifest within the Earth Plane as dense matter. You experience the Astral Body through your dream state. Everything is a dream before it becomes a reality. All the realities of your past, your present, and your future live within the Astral Body. The Astral Body holds every experience you have ever had, or will ever have, in your physical, dense form. It holds the records that sum up your Whole Energy. In other words, you are experiencing on another plane of consciousness within the Astral Plane moments before you experience in the physical. It is what your "de-ja vu" is all about. When you feel that what you are doing now you have done before (when your whole energy is sensing that which took place at another time is exactly how it is taking place in this moment), it is because the doorway to the Astral Plane was briefly open to your consciousness and you experienced twice that which took place first in the Astral Plane, then in the Physical Plane. As the doorway opened, your experience in the Astral Plane was immediately followed by the physical experience, so you consciously realized that this took place before but you could not know where or how. Look at it this way: your Astral Body is the rehearsal taking place before the performance, the performance being the physical, dense energy experiencing the dream.

The Astral Body is working in dream state to open the conscious mind to receive information from past and present lives, to examine fears and perceptions that block growth. It works to clear away the negative energy that limits your movement through the Earth Plane and blocks you from your God-self. The function of the Astral Body is to open to God's vibration and to unite with Spirit to serve your human Ego Be-ING, to awaken it to the power and Light that you are, in Truth. It is a delicate operation because each Be-ING within the Physical Plane holds great fear and negativity in the perception created through the Ego's manipulation of all your bodies....and you can clearly see a great deal of this negativity through the dream state. That is why you have disturbing dreams. You are acting out the fears in your Astral Body that direct you in your conscious state. Through acting out these fears the energy works to release them from your consciousness by transforming the fear into understanding on a deeper level of your Be-ING, a universal understanding that connects you to God, to the Whole of Life. So when you see violence, anger, all the negative emotions in your dream state, you are viewing the blocks that the Ego has created, and the Astral Body is working with Spirit to direct positive understanding of these emotions.

It is complicated for your Ego to understand what is being given here, only because the Ego resists in letting go of the fears that block it. Know this: you receive guidance in Astral Body (dream state) from your Spiritual Body. Many times you do not retain what takes place in dream state because your Ego is not ready to absorb the information through the conscious mind, yet it is experienced on a deep level where it begins to move energy throughout your Be-ING....and this movement of energy begins to put together the information needed by creating powerful symbols within the dream state that clarify the fears....for only that which is clear in your consciousness can be released, transformed, for it is the truth of this clarity that enables the Ego to release its hold, its gripping fear, from your Be-ING.

There are many different types of dreams, for you dream on many levels. At the highest level you are connecting to your God-self, you are given clear instruction and you are clearly being worked on and healed by the Angelic Realm. At the gross level you are directly experiencing your physical existence by creating similar situations with people who are in your life, and you relive your day with them through your dream state. They are called vivid dreams, for you clearly understand them as they unfold like a story. These dreams serve you to re-experience in order to receive a clear picture of where your attention is in your a-wake state. Then there are the dreams in camouflage and confusion. Here is where your deepest fears are hidden. Energy trapped in the Physical Body translates into these dreams. They are wanting to be found, brought to the surface, so they can be healed, balanced and released from your Physical Be-ING.

The Astral Body is working as an Archaeologist, digging the buried treasures of your past, for everything in this state comes from your total Be-ING, meaning past life experiences, as well as present life. All exists within this state- hence the confusion.... and as the Archaeologist of your Astral Body digs up the past, it works with the Spiritual Body to connect the past to the present so you are able then to make sense and reason out of where you are and what is blocking you in this life. Therefore, your Astral Body plays a major part in assisting the Whole of your Be-ING by putting the pieces of the puzzle together, working independently from the Ego, so there can be no distortion at this level of your energy. Ask your questions on this Body and you will be assisted further in your understanding.

Q. What is the purpose of the rehearsal that takes place in the Astral Body?

All precaution is taken so you may have many opportunities to create balance and begin to recognize your God energy. Within the Astral Body you are protected from your Ego Body. Your Spiritual Body enters and Higher Guidance comes through to direct you in the creation of your a-wake state. One of the functions of the Astral Body is to rehearse the experience that you are creating before you manifest it into the solid, dense matter within the Physical Plane. An example of this is: if your Ego is battling, telling your boss that he has been unfair and you want him to rectify a situation or you will leave your job, in your Astral Body you will play this out many times before it manifests in a physical form. You may dream in your dream state that you tell him abruptly and he violently reacts. This is your energy rehearsing in order to create the balanced and desired outcome. It may rehearse this many times in many different ways before you actually create in physical form the steps you take in this situation. This precaution is taken because your Ego Body is fearful.

If your Ego were on its own without the Astral Body to intervene, fear would block your movement at every turn. Nothing would be accomplished in a positive way. This `rehearsal` is to lend courage to your Ego so it may step aside allowing your creative force (God-self) to manifest the outcome. There are times that negativity is manifested even though a rehearsal takes place. This is because the Ego fear is so powerful that it penetrates the Astral Plane and distorts what it is receiving from the Higher Spiritual Body. In this case the Ego is in deep sleep-state, which creates denial and fear that equals negative existence filled with corruption and despair.

Q. I had an experience while I was walking through Central Park with a friend, a sensation of watching from above the two of us walking in the park. I actually felt myself floating above us as we were walking. This happened at a very difficult time in my life. Can you tell me what took place?

Your Astral Body exited the physical while you were within a conscious state, and in that moment you were able to view both bodies at once. Your depression and lack of love for self, created deep despair, so deep that the mechanism of the Astral Body was triggered in order to assist your whole Be-ING in raising your energy out of the darkness you had created.

When a person falls into deep darkness and the Ego has consumed, with its perception of fear, all of the Light, your God-self enters your consciousness to relieve the pain and darkness enough for you to turn around the downward spiral of your energy. It is a built-in survival mechanism. When it fails, it is because your darkness was maintained for too long a period of earth time, this being your choice on another level of your Be-ING. We will speak about this level at a different time. Here you used your God Power to save yourself from being consumed by your Ego Body's fear.

Q. Is it possible for us to direct what we want to happen from the Astral Plane so that it will manifest on the Earth Plane?

You direct everything in your life. You are the Creator. The assistance of your Astral Body is all part of your essence. It is of your Higher vibration, for you are all One (God), in truth….and you are directing all of your energy except for the Ego. Your Ego is out of alignment and tries to direct your other bodies by interfering with their movement; and that is the reason you have difficulty manifesting what you desire, in truth. The Ego blocks your true instincts, so your true instincts do not come through. Many times you are manifesting only through the Ego perception. Your Astral Body is working to prepare you to receive your true identity, but you must walk through the darkness of your Ego in order to learn of and receive your Higher-self. Once your Higher-self is recognized through your whole Be-ING and exists within your conscious state, the Ego then cannot interfere; you are then within your power, within your God-self. So you must trust that whatever you create, whether created through your Ego Body or your Spiritual Body, it is correct. It is what you need within the moment in order to awaken the sleeping Be-ING.

4. THE EMOTIONAL BODY

The fourth body is called the Emotional Body. At this point, the people in my group began to feel a little more comfortable with the idea of exploring the Emotional Body because the emotions are something that we can relate to, we experience them, they are the most powerful part of our experience in Physical Body. But it was a surprise when we all discovered how important, how powerful, our Emotional Body is and how the perception held through our Ego distorts our emotions. It was a surprise to find out that our emotions are manipulated by the fear that we hold through our Ego Body. I am sure that you feel your emotions are true and they <u>are</u>: true to the <u>Ego</u>. But you will begin to see that they are not pure because they are manipulated, motivated, through fear. Let us continue now by listening to what ASTRA taught us about the Emotional Body.

*It is because you are working through the Ego Body's perception that the emotions are distorted in each Be-ING on the Earth Plane, for your emotions are directed through fear and lack of trust. In reality, the emotions are your teacher; they are here to teach you of your true identity. The Emotional Body is where you experience your life in physical form. You experience through the distorted, fearful emotions of the Ego or you experience through your fearless God-self. Most Be-ings on the Earth Plane are experiencing their emotions through the Ego Body. When you are within an emotion you are expressing a feeling that is passing through you, and your feelings are mostly fearful for the Ego directs fear into every experience; it is the food, the fuel, that keeps the Ego in control of all the other bodies. Because you are in fear you do not allow yourself to receive from your Higher-consciousness, from your true identity, your God- self. Fear motivates you and you experience the physical life in a sleep-state, for the fear energy puts the consciousness into an altered state of being and you are, therefore, not wakeful in the Emotional Body.

It is difficult for Be-ings on the Earth Plane to understand how to rise above emotion and to perceive it without fear. To clearly rise above your Emotional Body you must begin to allow the emotions to be the teacher to your whole Be-ING, for they will guide you into consciousness. This becomes complicated at its beginning, for you would believe that if the emotions are within fear how could you then be taught by this fear. **You are taught through the fear that is being experienced within your Emotional Body.** You will begin to see more clearly where you are to focus your energy in order to learn from the experiences created out of the emotional Body.

By experiencing your emotions and experiencing what manifests in physical form through your emotional state you are able to see clearly where you are in truth in relation to your God-self. When Be-ings on the Earth Plane create war, this is due to an emotional understanding of the situation as well as a mental picture of what is taking place; yet the true motivation for creating the war is coming from the fear manifested in the Emotional Body. This motivates Be-ings on the Earth Plane to separate from their Higher-consciousness and to create the war in order to protect them from the fear that is held within their Be-ING. The Ego manipulates the Emotional Body, for when a Be- ING is fearful for his survival his emotions become powerful and he is pulled into a negative warfare, not only within his Physical Body but also within his world.

This is how man continues to create the decay of his surroundings....through his emotional outbursts of fear.

It is important to become conscious when these outbursts take place, for only through consciousness will you be able to release the fear and focus on what is manifesting in truth. This will allow you to be motivated by your God-self and eliminate great negativity and devastation within your Earth Plane. Your actions are not truthful when they are coming from the emotional turmoil created out of your Ego perceptions.

The Emotional Body is a complicated vibration within your Be-ING for it has great power over how you structure your whole reality. Emotions are the brushes that stroke the canvas with their colors (their perceptions). The canvas is the unlimited space given to you to create God's image on the Earth Plane. The choices made through the emotions are powerful. You must learn how to accept the emotions and to experience the lessons that are taught within each emotion.

To be a prisoner of the emotions is to become your emotions. This is meaning that you, in your unconscious state, are captured by your emotions. This is why there is so much violence, war, cruelty, and pain....because Be-ings are motivated by pure emotion and there is no balance with the other bodies for making positive choices. When you have had the experience of blind rage, for example, you have experienced being captured by the emotion; the word `blind` meaning unconscious of what is in truth....only seeing the darkness, the fury, the fear that you hold at that moment within your Be-ING. When a person strikes out at another with violent emotion it is because he holds the most devastating fear within his Be-ING, and he is captured by that feeling and motivated to destroy that which within his perception is standing in his way of peace. This sounds very psychological but in truth it is a simple reality of how your Emotional Body is directed through the perception of fear held by your Ego Body. The degree varies within each Be-ING only because some Be-ings have more balance within their seven bodies than others; yet even those with this balance are being directed in the Emotional Body through the fear of extinction (death) that the Ego perception carries in this Plane.

You must begin to pay more attention to the emotions in order to see more clearly the Ego's influence and interference in your wholeness, in your power, as a God Be-ING (a creative force). Many Be-ings on the Earth Plane can learn much about the emotions through the art of `Theatre,` for within theater there is freedom to explore the emotions, to watch what takes place within the Emotional Body, and to have complete control over what is manifested through the emotions. All Be-ings must learn how to watch the emotions in order to be enlightened by the situation that is created from the experience. Ask your questions here and you will be assisted further in understanding the Emotional Body.

Q. How are our Emotional Bodies the same? And how do they differ between individuals?

Each Be-ING expresses his emotions based on the degree of understanding that exists in his soul vibration; in other words, the accumulation of experiences throughout past lives and this life, for as the emotional experience is the teacher it is solely dependent upon the types of experiences and how they are absorbed into the consciousness. Remember, the emotions are your teacher. Many times you are taught without being aware of the teaching; yet you change, grow, from the experience which indicates the lesson has been learned. The difference is within the accumulation of experiences that have been forceful enough to elevate your consciousness. This is meaning that because you are in a sleep-state the experiences that are forceful are the ones which will awaken you and thereby elevate your consciousness. You have many experiences in every moment. Most of them do not alter your state of sleep because they are repeated patterns of behavior that are automatically relived through your Emotional Body.

Q. You have said that sometimes people need body work to remove Karma from the cells of the body. Does the Emotional Body carry Karma that needs to be released?

Karma is stored within the physical. The experience of the emotions creates action of Karma and the memory is stored within the cells of the Physical Body. Memories from past life experiences are stored within the cells of your Be-ING, along with the child memories of the present life. The Emotional Body's function is to interpret the feelings that pass through your Be-ING. During the experience, if you are within fear, blocks will be created in your energy field, and these blocks are stored within the cells. You carry them with you from lifetime to lifetime until you are able to bring the experience to the surface and relive it in wakeful state creating a balance in which the energy is freed. It is important to understand the concept of energy for you are energy, your thoughts are energy and all you experience is energy. When you are within fear, you block the experience. Blocking the energy creates decay of the physical.

Q. When I have difficulty in connecting with my emotions, is that due to the Ego? What causes this difficulty?

It is the Ego's perception that is blocking the experience of emotions that carry a great weight of fear behind them. For example, if you had in many past lives experienced devastation through love, you would have great fear in expressing love in this life. Your emotions would be distorted by the Ego's perception of love.

You have brought to yourself a negative lesson about love wherein you suffered loss in your past-life experiences, and pain and fear were created….what happened here is that the Ego's perception created a sense of lack within your Be-ING which told you that you were not worthy of receiving love. With this information you blocked out positive experiences of love. When you are working in the present life to come into the Light and draw in a positive love relationship, you must go through the pain of your old perception….or the fear will become greater and that fear will block you from expressing the love that you feel within your Be-ING.

The work here is to relive through dream state or meditation or spiritual healing the past negative experiences and to be wakeful enough within them to change what you see and begin to see the truth, that the love partner of the past also had fear and was being motivated by his fear….what blocks your energy is the sleep-state that you fall into because of the fear generated by the Ego. The Ego is a selfish entity and only sees its own pain, cannot see beyond itself. That is why distortion takes place in relationships. Only when you are wakeful can you see the oneness of your Be-ING and recognize the sameness within the partner. When you are able to see his fear you are able to recognize how to pass through the fear together and come into the Light of forgiveness and love.

Q. Is it always the Ego that blocks the emotions?

Yes. It is always the Ego that blocks you from God. You may think of the Ego as the fallen Angel, for all your bodies are Heavenly bodies. You were created and manifested by the Creator. The Ego is the Body that fell out of alignment with your other six bodies. It fell into darkness and fear was created, loss of memory came into the Mental Body, confusion penetrated the Emotional Body, a disconnection from other worlds took place in the Astral Body and sickness befell the Physical Body, then power was blocked from the Spiritual Body. All of this took place when the Ego Body fell out of alignment; and in this life the work is to realign the Ego so fear will fall away from your consciousness and the path to God will open and you will become who you are in Truth, a manifestation of God.

Q. Are acting classes helpful to people who are fearful of experiencing their emotions?

If you are not able to act out an emotion you are blocking a great deal of energy and you are pulling it deeper into the cells of your Be-ING, creating decay within your Physical Body. It is extremely important to use whatever tools that are available to help you experience your emotions, to act them out. Acting lessons are greatly helpful, especially to young children in releasing emotions that can be threatening, because the acting out of their emotions in play form frees them to experience fear, anger and all negative feelings that usually create a strain within them. Through play acting they learn to release fear, by transforming the energy. This creates a strength that enables them to deal with feelings that once crippled them in their existence. Adults benefit as well as long as they are connected to playing, to acting out for the sake of performance. If they are not, then they must take a different road, work through dream therapy, physical therapy, and spiritual therapy, where they can learn to release trapped emotions and express them in a safe environment. These are some of the ways to assist the frightened Ego in coming back into alignment with your other Bodies.

Q. Is there an exercise that you could give us that would assist our getting in tune with our Emotional Bodies?

Become more aware of your Emotional Body and be more watchful while in an emotional vibration. You must learn to watch your emotions as if you were watching someone else within an emotional upset. You must learn to detach from your own emotion in order not to become captured by the emotion. Use the watchful energy of your God-self to separate enough from the experience of the emotion in order to see it more clearly and penetrate the lesson being taught through the Emotional Body....meaning, when you can watch yourself within an emotional state you can begin to see the fear that is motivating the emotion....and only when you can see the fear operating can you separate from it and redirect the experience into a wakeful encounter. It takes time, patience, and great love of your own Be-ING to be able to see your emotions more clearly, to reach the core that motivates them, and free yourself from the Ego's fear.

5. THE MENTAL BODY

The Mental Body came next for discussion. What we think, what we feel, how we react….you would believe that all of this would be in alignment; but as we all know, what we think and what we feel can be very opposite from one another. What we do does not always reflect the mind or the emotion. That is how divided our energies are. That to me is the proof that we are out of alignment and that some 'mad' energy has control of our Be-ing. As you hear what is being said by the Guardian Angel, (ASTRA) on the Mental Body, pay attention to the power that you possess in this Body and how the Ego Body devours this power. Now we shall hear ASTRA.

*The Mental Body is the Body that creates all of manifestation. That is why you are working to focus into your God-mind, for the Mental Body is divided in energy due to the Ego's greatest interference in this Body. The Ego-mind is the part of your Be-ING that perceives in darkness all of creation. The God-mind is the part of your Be-ING that perceives creation within the Light. The Mental Body, in truth, manifests all thought forms and you experience them first within this Body and then again throughout your other bodies when the thought is manifested into the Physical Plane.

Thoughts create life….all aspects of life are created through the mental energy; the Ego manipulates the mind and thoughts become dark and fearful, creating separation from the God-mind. Just as positive and negative energies exist in all of the manifestations that you experience in the Earth Plane, so does the negative force of the Ego exist most predominantly in the Mental Body. Your mind in the Earth Plane is challenged by the negative pull of the Ego's perception, for you are in a field of gravity and dense matter. This entrapment is also the blessing that motivates the Ego to follow the desire within your Be-ING to fly beyond the gravity.

The negativity of your Ego perceptions motivates your whole Be-ING to connect to your God-mind, in truth, for your creative energy is in constant battle to be free from the confinements of this gravity, of this pull, of this dense vibration. You are Be-ings with two minds and you are in conflict, you are within battle of Light and dark energies. This entrapment was created by your God-self in order to manifest motivation towards movement out of the confinement, for energy is what you are and energy is eternally in movement. When it becomes trapped it creates decay.

Your body decays when energies are trapped in conflict of mind at any given point within the Physical, Mental or Emotional Bodies. The reason it decays when trapped is that energy, in order to be a living vibration, must be in constant movement. Entrapment, therefore, is like stagnated water. If water is stagnated, it decays and no longer is useful, nurturing. All energy works exactly the same. If you, through your Ego perception within your Mental Body, see yourself as weak, you shall trap energy in this perception and become weak and decay your energy at that point. You may place the weakness in your physical ability, and the body becomes weak, holding this trapped energy (these thought patterns) within it. You trap your energy only when you are within Ego perception….for fear is what traps movement of energy….for it creates blockage.

You were created to elevate mind and to experience your own creations in the physical world; in order to do this, you created a vessel (the Physical Body) in which to house your energy, trapping part of your energy for a period of time in the Earth Plane for the purpose of generating more mental energy to ensure the Eternal Existence of the Creator; yet at this time in your evolution you are trapping your mental energy more and more through the Ego-mind….the perceptions of the Ego have become the power in the Earth Plane and your mental energy is dangerously tilting towards decay of the whole of Creation.

You must begin to see more clearly the power of consciousness and you must begin to see how you have been creating through sleep-state, in order to understand that within the Ego perception you are not conscious; yet the God-self from within continues to strive in elevating your energy and bringing it into consciousness. At this point, your mind is divided. You are weakening the Creative Force through this division. The memory of who you are is lost and you are seeking to discover the truth: **that you create through mind and you manifest what you think and you experience yourself in the way that you think of yourself.** Thoughts create patterns and these patterns are powerful energy fields that move bodies of vibration (electrical force fields of matter) into shapes and substances that form your physical existence, your physical world.

You must begin to see more clearly that when you are within Ego-mind you are creating illusion, you are stepping away from Truth and into a fantasy that is filled with fear and despair, for it separates you from the power of Truth which is present in your God-mind. The fear that motivates the Ego traps the God force (your energy) and creates your extinction. Ask your questions on the Mental Body and you shall be assisted further.

Q. Can you tell us how we can be more creative with our minds? Is there an exercise or method that we can use to gain control?

The Mental Body is always moving for you are always thinking. Creation is happening in every moment. The mind creates. Many thoughts pass through your mind....pictures, fantasies....all of these thoughts are energy and they exist within the Mind of God. The mind automatically moves on its own power. It moves with thoughts of past lives as well as thoughts of future and present. You cannot control the complex energy. You must allow the energy to flow by allowing thoughts to pass in front of you and then away. When you focus your attention (your consciousness) on any thought you empower that thought and it is created into your life. The thought is manifested first in mind then held in the Astral Plane where it awaits the time where all elements are perfectly aligned for its manifestation into the Earth Plane. This is why negative thoughts created in the present may not manifest into the Earth Plane immediately but rather take years or a lifetime to do so.

The power of thought is immeasurable. Picture your mind as a camera. **You spot a thought through the lens of mind and put the Light of Consciousness upon it**. The moment you do this you empower the thought by manifesting it. Thoughts manifest your world from within and from without. You are the creator of these thoughts. As the creator, whatever thought you bring into consciousness you must confront and experience in physical form....and through the experience you must come to an understanding, a balancing of energy. That is another reason why you repeat lifetime after lifetime the same negative thought patterns and manifest them into your reality- because you have not found the balance, the teachings, within them; and until you become conscious of how your thought patterns affect all of creation, you will continue to create Karma, which is your lesson.

You may use this exercise to assist you in quieting runaway thoughts: meditation, for meditation is the tool to releasing the Ego's fear from your present moment. As you are in meditation, you are exercising the mind to let go of all thought patterns, which means that the thoughts no longer take up the space of consciousness. What is within this space of meditation is silence, space, peace, and God-mind. During meditation there is a cleansing that is taking place, a healing of spirit and emotion....for within the emptiness there is the sound of Truth, the presence of Power, the guidance of your God-self. You must learn to meditate each day, twice within it, at sunrise and sunset; and this exercise will serve you greatly in opening to your God-consciousness.

Q. When we want to manifest that which we believe to be our true desire, is it enough to see the result or must we picture each step in the progression to manifestation?

You must take each step because a misstep can result in a completely different manifestation. Example: in the acting profession each moment creates the next. You cannot from the first moment skip over the next five moments and expect to create the desired outcome because each moment always creates the next....it builds, as a symphony builds from one note to the next. You change the whole complexion of that which you desire when you are careless with your moment. As you are creating that which you desire from the deepest part

of your Be-ING, you must acknowledge the Creator God....
for what you receive is not always what you believe you desire,
for most of your desires come through your Ego perception.
What you receive will come from your God-self as long as you
are conscious of each moment you are in. Then your God- self
will create your true desire....that which you need, that which
brings you into Conscious state.

*Q. Many people in the last few generations have been focusing
on the destruction of this planet through environmental damage,
nuclear war, etc., When so many people focus on destruction, could
they manifest it?*

When you focus your Ego-consciousness on a thought, you are
manifesting that thought. You are creating your deepest fears
when you are obsessed with them. In preventing destruction,
the perception needs to shift into a desire to heal the planet.
Your Ego sees the world blowing up....your God self sees the
world illuminated with love. The mind is focused in Truth
on preventing such disasters. Even the Ego deeply desires to
prevent destruction of the Earth Plane, for the Ego fears its
own death and, therefore, for its own preservation it unites
with your Higher self to preserve the planet. **The Ego desiring
to preserve out of fear and the God-self desiring to preserve
out of love**....and only in this desire to preserve does the Ego
unite with your God-self.

The true destruction to your planet comes from the greed
of the Ego, the Ego's desire to take, strip, and possess is the
dangerous energy of the Earth Plane and the true cause of its
destruction, for the Ego's thoughts are focused in possessing
for the Ego's physical self. The material greed and the worship

of the material world that the Ego holds, is what will decay the planet. That is why you must bring the Ego into alignment with your God-self. The true destruction is within the perception and the perception is now within greed and fear of material loss. Know that within this focus you are in <u>loss</u> of your True self.

6. The Ego Body

This body is the one that we've been hearing about all along; when we spoke of the Mental Body, when we spoke of the Emotional Body, the Ego Body was mentioned. We were all anxious to hear about this body because we then knew that the Ego Body was a powerful force in our lives, just how powerful was yet to be realized. I don't think any of us understand how gripping our Ego bodies can be or how damaging to our ability to live a happy, balanced life. Living with the Ego is like living with two personalities. We learned that we are Be-ings of conflicting perceptions, conflicting desires, conflicting actions, as if two individuals were occupying one body. I am sure that you can recall in your memory a moment when you felt confused and pulled in opposite directions over issues of great importance in your life and at that moment feeling powerless and so off- balance that you believed yourself to be crazed and unable to cope. That is a direct result of our Ego Body's power over our existence in this Physical Plane.

I don't mean for this to sound as though I believe we're all crazy, unable to function, for you know that would not be true. We are people who function very well within our Ego perception, meaning very well within the expectations of the Ego Plane, for we have all learned how to survive within this perception. So when we argue that, 'I'm successful,` 'I make a great deal of money,' 'I have* *power,' 'I have friendships and family,' 'I have a good time in this life' and `I don't feel divided,` it is because our Ego has succeeded in manipulating our energy to serve it in the material plane. This does not mean just because we feel content with our life that we are <u>within Truth;</u> what <u>is</u> meant is that the Ego creates a smoke screen around the mind and fills the consciousness with its set, structured ideas of what happiness means and what we need to obtain it in the material world in order to feel safe and secure.

When people feel negative about themselves and have feelings of failure, and poverty and sickness manifest in their lives, they are living a belief system created by the Ego's perception, which is: `if you cannot be successful in the structure which the Ego holds as an earth consciousness, then you must be the opposite and you must possess the Ego's formula of punishment for not succeeding.` What most of us do not understand is that we are serving an illusion in this perception. We are not serving our Higher consciousness. We are not serving the Whole of humanity. We are serving a <u>very minute portion of the Whole.</u> We are serving the little `me,` the small self, and we are completely unconscious of everything that exists around us, for we only see our own greed, our own pain, our own desires to obtain the great illusion of the Ego; and, ultimately, this divides us from our true self and each other. It divides us and conquers our energy, so we fall and consequently `fail` in this experience called `life.`

Do not misinterpret that because I am saying our Ego happiness is an illusion that we must give it up. We are not being asked to give up anything. I am speaking about adding to what we already know and have experienced. I am speaking about our limited perceptions and how much more we are, in Truth. These teachings are here to assist us in tapping into our Higher-consciousness (God-self) and adding that light to what we already possess, for that is the great purpose of our existence in this lifetime. We are all here at a specific time, coming into the millennium where the structure and the inner wisdom of each of us will surface and change the world (universe) as we now know it, so stay with me and hear the words of ASTRA, the Guardian Angel, that were spoken on the subject of the Ego Body as follows:

*The Ego Body is the Body that rules the Earth Plane in that this Body holds the illusion of the physical earth together and creates a stage on which your God-self (the Creator) experiences the creation in dense matter (solid form). That is because the belief that the Ego holds in the physical is what holds the dense energy together. As you were told, all things are created out of mind. If the belief in the material were not present in the Ego perception, the structure of the material world, as you know it, would not be present. It would fade like a picture that loses its vividness and color, so your material world would fade in and out of focus because the belief system that it is real would not be in place. **The earth is a mental energy manifested in the projection of the thought that preceded it, this is what the earth is.** Thus the Ego is a powerful body, for its belief in the illusion creates and holds the material substances within your plane together.

As the Ego serves in this way, it also blocks Truth because the Ego perception has created many more illusions in order to keep the Truth from entering the consciousness, fearing that the Truth would destroy the manifested illusion, would take away the ingredient that holds the physical world together in which case the Ego would die. The fear of death is what drives the Ego within every Be-ING. This belief in death holds your Ego in constant pursuit of power and the desire to control everything in the physical creation. The result of its belief in death is the power that motivates the Ego in all you experience in the physical plane. You may picture the Ego as Lucifer from your scriptures, for it is! This negative energy is obsessed with itself in the illusion and continuously creates blocks to your God-self (your true power). The Ego is the `child` of your Be-ING. Your God-self is also present within the human form in order to experience the physical creation. That is why your God-mind shares space with your Ego-mind within your physical Be-ING.

Although many Be-ings do not realize that the mind is being occupied by two perceptions (that of the God-consciousness and that of Ego-consciousness), it is so! Most often the Ego-mind is blocking the God-mind from your consciousness, for it is holding your whole energy prisoner to the fear it creates within the whole of humanity, within the whole experience of the dense energy and physical matter. `Gravity` is meaning heavy vibration. It is the heavy fear perception that ensures the Ego's power in the physical experience. As gravity holds you in solid form on the earth, so does the Ego hold your mind in its power through the gravity of fear that it creates. When you begin to see the Light of your True self as a manifestation of God (the Creator) you will begin to see the Ego as a frightened child, constantly demanding attention; and you will learn how to ease and eliminate the fear of this child that so deeply influences your experiences within this manifested illusion.

Before you can take charge of this child within your own Be-ING, you must first acknowledge that the Ego exists as the part of your Be-ING that holds all of your fears and negativity, all of your judgments and misguided actions....and that you have the adult part of your Be-ING which is your God-self waiting to take charge and free you from the illusion that you are now trapped within.

Therefore, what is reality? There are many realities for there are many perceptions, and each one holds his perception as a reality. This does not mean that because you call something a reality that it is real. Coming to the place where you begin to see that, that which you call a reality is an illusion and what you are feeling is fear enables you to open to receive the guidance that is within you, that is within every Be-ING.... for every Be-ING is a Manifestation of God.

Be-ings of the Earth Plane are working now to heal their pain and fears through psychotherapy, which has been created in order for man to hear himself, to hear his own Ego speak. As man is in his therapy and he is speaking he begins to listen and he hears his Ego. This assists him in healing many false realities; yet it is not enough, for once you erase a false reality there is nothing to fill the empty space. What is needed to fill that space with true reality is you're God-self-to become conscious of your God-self. To be conscious of the Whole is to begin recognizing that you are the Creator and that you have the power to transform the fearful child called `Ego` into a powerful adult (watchman/guard) of the Earth Plane.

Your Ego, however, continues to keep you in sleep-state, it is the master manipulator. It creates false realities and it creates needs that block out your desire to seek the God within. You must begin to learn more and more about yourself as energy. You must begin to see your connection to all that exists, as `One energy` in order for each of you to be open to receive the guidance and love of your God-self. We shall speak more about your Ego in order for you to recognize it more readily than you now do. At this point, ask your questions on the Ego Body.

Q. Is the story in the Bible of the fallen Angel Lucifer, a parable about the separation of our Ego Body from our other bodies?

Yes. The Ego holds all negative vibration. The Devil, as you imagine it, does not exist. The Ego, when out of alignment (its present state in your plane), is the Devil. It is your worst enemy. It destroys relationships, countries, the animal kingdom, communication, the atmosphere, and so forth. All destruction comes from your Ego. `The Devil lives within.`

Q. In other words, we must balance the Ego because we will never really be rid of it, and maybe we don't want to be rid of it because the Ego does have some beneficial functions. Is this correct?

You do not want to lose your Ego but rather transform it, enabling it to operate in its proper perspective which is to oversee your other bodies. It is the watchman within your Be-ING. When all Bodies are in alignment the Ego is in its proper perspective and is able to orchestrate occurrences taking place within the other bodies of your Be-ING.

You have learned through centuries and many lifetimes to focus on the Ego, to have greed for the self. This long-time focus on your Ego has empowered it. Once you remove the focus and disperse it throughout your other bodies, then the Ego will take its proper position. To accomplish this, it is necessary that you learn to focus in every moment. To do this, you must possess the knowledge that you are the Creator and you are <u>all</u> that exists; therefore, there is no desperate need within your Be-ING to possess anything, no object, no other Be-ING, nor power over anything. You accept exactly where you are because you know you lack nothing.

Your Ego feeds on a sense of lack, on the idea that you need something from without to make you feel whole. It feeds on the illusion that you need the `material` for your identity. It feeds mostly on the idea that you <u>are</u> your Body. The Ego's first place of great attack is the Physical Body because it is of gross matter which is not sensitive in its vibration and, therefore, an easy target. The Ego enters the mind and tells your Be-ING that this is all there is, that you <u>are</u> your Body. There are many Karmic repercussions to this belief because it tells you that you are how you look. For example, if you lack physical beauty you will not be loved, with an imperfect body you have nothing (if you lose your leg you cease to exist).

These beliefs are all untruths, for you are <u>not</u> your Body. It is very important that you learn this lesson because it is in the Physical Body where you must first release the Ego's hold. Using meditation can assist you because in that space you are free of your Physical Body and are connecting to your Heavenly Bodies. Meditation is a tool for awakening your Be-ING to your True self and freeing you from your sleep-state. The Physical Body comes into a more alert, wakeful state as a result of meditation.

Q. It is my understanding that the Third Eye seems to be the more psychic Chakra. Can you explain why the Ego is in that Chakra?

The Third Eye is your watchman position. It is the place from where you evaluate. The Third Eye sees beyond the Physical

Plane, while the Ego sees within the Physical Plane. The Ego refuses to allow the other bodies to operate independently by interfering with them; and that is why many people cannot open their Third Eye and go beyond their physical sight. Only an Ego that is aligned can open to see beyond. It depends on the perception of the Be-ING. If a Be-ING is in Ego perception, the Third Eye will be closed and the Ego will only permit the material view of the world into the consciousness. When the Ego is aligned and you are within God perception, the Third Eye is open and you are connected to the Creator and see beyond the physical, material world. Because the Ego Energy is at the Third Eye Chakra there are very few Be-ings who can see beyond their material needs. It is the position for the Ego because when your Ego is aligned it guards the energy beyond the physical, it stands at the gateway bringing forth the God-consciousness, then your whole world changes visually as well as emotionally.

Q. Is it similar to when someone has an alignment with his Ego and projects a feeling of calm and patience about his person?

This is how you can recognize a Be-ING who is within the Light, for there is not only calmness and patience in him, also an acceptance in his nature....for only through acceptance can one open to his Spiritual Body. It takes great patience to accept and to trust. Once you begin to open, to receive from your Higher-consciousness, you will transform into a loving, patient, accepting energy....and your Ego will be in alignment, no longer interfering with your True identity.

Q. Does the Ego manipulate the other Bodies? Let's say, the Mental Body has thoughts that it would not normally have or focus on. Is this due to the Ego's manipulation?

The Ego always manipulates the Mental Body. Very few of your thoughts are pure. Pure thought comes from the Spiritual energy (the God energy). Although you are of two minds (God-mind and Ego-mind), within this dense plane most of your thoughts come from your Ego-mind. The Ego has captured the material world, and, therefore, seizes all of your thought patterns and turns them into physical desires, greed, fear, and so forth. It creates a great cloud over your God-mind, and your work is to lift the cloud that separates you from your `Higher` vibration.

Q. Can we quiet our thoughts? For example, there are times when we have many thoughts racing through our minds, and we say to ourselves---`stop.` At this point, can we ask for and expect to receive knowledge from a quiet place?

In order to receive knowledge, you must be within a quiet space. You must eliminate the racing of thoughts. It is necessary to become conscious of the moment that you are in. This brings you into a wakeful state where your Ego cannot interfere; so when you ask for knowledge in your conscious state, you shall receive it. It may not come in an instant as you might expect. It may come through an experience that will teach you your answer; but when you are conscious you are also patient and you trust that the answer will come-and it does.

Q. Does asking in that way circumvent the Ego? Am I understanding it correctly, that we have to arrive at a point where we must be able to see our Ego and push it aside?

That is correct. You can only transform your Ego when you are able to clearly see it in operation when you realize that you are completely within Ego, and in that instant of realization you stop, quiet the mind, come into consciousness, and ask to receive guidance from your God-self. You can only transform the Ego within the moment, for there is only the moment…. and you are transforming your Ego in every moment when you are conscious and aware of both its presence and its negative interference in your life.

Q. What do you mean when you say the Ego is the watchman, what is it's true function?

The True Function of your Ego is to assess all that comes through your other bodies, meaning when you have an emotional reaction to something the Ego stands outside of the emotion and watches it unfold, in order to create space for your Spiritual body to enter and illuminate the truth in the situation. When the Ego is in alignment, you are never captured by the illusions directed to you from Be-ings that are within Ego perception. Because the Ego is connected to the material, it is the `best evaluator` of what is coming through the dense matter into your aura, and only when it is in alignment with your God-self can it truly serve you.

Q. With an aligned Ego don't we risk becoming passive people? Are not passive people a target for the more aggressive Ego minded?

You are confusing passive with lack of power. In your Ego world Be-ings believe that to be kind is a weakness, and to be giving is a weakness. Therefore, when you see a Be-ING in alignment with his compassionate perception you think he is passive and will be overpowered. This is not what you are becoming. When in alignment you are powerful, more powerful than the aggressive Ego, for you are not trapped within a perception of greed, you are open to receive what is presented in the moment. What does this mean? It means through acceptance of what is you are able to create what you need in the moment and by receiving what you need, you are free to draw from the Light all the power and wisdom of your God-self, therefore, passive becomes powerful.

7. THE SPIRITUAL BODY

We all began to realize that because the Ego Body is so powerful we have much work to do in order to fulfill our dedication to spiritual growth....our dedication to aligning ourselves with God. We understood that we are very complicated people and that each one of us holds the key to unraveling the Ego perception and creating a true connection to our Higher-self. So by this time, we were looking forward to hearing directly from ASTRA about our true nature, our Spiritual Body.

The Spiritual body is the seventh Body and it resides in the Crown Chakra. From our Crown Chakra we draw in the vital energy that keeps us alive in Spirit and connected to our True self, and the quality of our lives depends upon how much Light we draw in through our Crown Chakra. The more powerful the Ego perception, the less Light can penetrate through our Crown Chakra and fill our physical bodies. This realization prompted all of us to work on our Chakra, cleanse them, and visualize the Light coming into them. We were taught by ASTRA how to maintain our Chakra. We are energy; therefore, we are light, we are color, sound and vibration. We were taught how to use the color energy needed within each Chakra in order to maintain and open each Chakra, for it is there where our seven bodies reside. If we are weak, for example, in the Emotional Body, that Chakra is blocked with energy created *from the interference of the Ego's perception. When we are <u>within</u> <u>consciousness,</u> we are aware of the Ego's presence and we are aware of Chakra and how to cleanse them and fill them with Light so that the **Eternal Energy** of which we are composed continues to flow.*

At this point, I wish to share with you ASTRA'S description of our most `magnificent body,` our Spiritual Body.

*Your Spiritual Body is the umbilical cord that connects you on the Physical Plane to your True self, (the Creator God). The best way to describe this is that as you are within your Physical Body, you are also with the Creator God. You never leave the point of creation, in truth. Your energy is always `One` with God. The Physical Body is a reflection of the One manifested in physical form, and the Spiritual Body is the Light that comes through your Crown/Chakra and ignites your Be-ING with the love energy. The Love Energy is what holds the One together. Without it there is no manifestation of peace or joy, as you now know it in your Earth Plane. It is your Spiritual Body that keeps you in the arms of God.

Understand what spirit means: it means emotion, feeling…. it means High consciousness, joy….it is within a total love perception. This is the part of your Be-ING that has memory of the Creator….this is the part of your Be-ING that is the creative force within the Earth Plane. It is your Highest ideal, your Highest desire, to serve the Whole….it is the Light that shines through all of the dense vibration, the Light that comes into the mind when the mind is heavy and dark with fear…. it is the Light that you see within the tunnel….the Light that you search for within your pain….it is always with you. It is only blocked from your consciousness through the Ego's perception and attachment to the Physical Body and material world. Yet it is the spark that ignites all that exists, and that is why it is always available to you in your darkest hour.

Many Be-ings call it God. Many Be-ings believe that it is something separate from themselves....and that they call to it to save them from themselves. They do not recognize that it is who they are that `they are the Light.` Those who recognize the Light within themselves move more quickly through the darkness in the Earth Plane. Their sufferings are short-lived in comparison to those within Ego perception; yet every living Be-ING is of the Spirit.... this is where your power lies. When you are able to align all of your bodies and you are connecting to your Spiritual Body, you are graced by wisdom and truth and deep love for all of creation which frees your entrapment within the physical....so you are able to create in God's image. The Be-ings within this Light are the Be-ings who have created all that is pure, all that is of the Light that exists in your earth. All the compassion and the love for mankind has come out of this Light....all of the diseases that have been cured have come out of this Light....all of the beauty that has been created through art has come out of this Light (Love) `the Spirit.`

In order to continue to grow brighter in the physical world, this alignment must manifest within each Be-ING. It is time to let go of your false images and see Truth, even though it is difficult for the Ego to accept that the truth is not within the physical form but is within a formless, shapeless vibration that is free to take any shape or form. The Ego only sees limited sparks of Truth on its journey in the Earth Plane; and in order for God to reign in this Plane the Ego must relinquish its fear. You are

God manifested in the Earth Plane and you must recognize this Truth so you may recognize your power to heal yourself.

In order to heal yourself, you must begin to see all of your bodies and clearly understand what blocks your energy in your perception and how to open to your God- self in order to release the negative emotions within the Emotional Body, the fears within the Mental Body, and the manipulating, selfish unconsciousness of the Ego Body. We are describing your energy on the Earth Plane in a manner in which your Ego can understand, for if you were given this information without the consideration of your fearful Ego perceptions you would remain trapped within the cycle that you are in on this Plane. Because it is a cycle that you are trapped within, you must return to the Earth over and over again. Until the cycle is broken and you are free of the density created through fear, you shall eternally remain a prisoner of this low plane of consciousness. We shall stop here and we will continue to work together on recognizing the many parts of your Be-ING so you may see them fit together as a Whole. You may now ask your questions on the Spiritual Body.

Q. Is the Soul the Spiritual Body?

Yes, the Soul and the Spirit are sparks of the God energy. A spark of energy, which is the Soul, is implanted very close to the `Heart/Chakra.` The Soul and Spirit are one. We separate them by name, however, so that you understand on which level we speak of the God Energy. We refer to the Soul when we speak of the Soul's purpose (experiencing/learning, and so forth), in the lower planes. We refer to Spirit, however, when we speak of the spark of your Higher-consciousness (the God energy) in the higher planes.

Q. How does the Spiritual Body relate to our being in the moment?

When seeking the moment, you must do so through aligning all of your bodies. When the state of alignment is achieved the Spiritual Body is present and it filters through your whole Being, creating balance and clarity in every moment. In order to connect to the God energy (the Spirit), you must do so through all of your bodies, focusing your energies in your Heart (your Center). You are in complete alignment when your attention and focus are at your Center. Whenever you are working through one body (for example, the Emotional Body), you are not aware of your other bodies because you become absorbed in your emotions. You are then out of balance, blocking the Spiritual Body from entering the Emotional Body. All perception becomes clouded with emotion preventing your ability to see Truth. It is important that you understand that all of your bodies are energy. All that exists is energy. You are working to balance your energies so that you are at a place of peace and joy, for only in this place of peace are you truly manifesting your God-self.

Q. It sounds to me that the Spiritual Body is rarely present in our other bodies, and, therefore, we are out of balance. Is this because the Ego is in control?

That is correct. You are rarely aware of your Spiritual Body because your Ego is slipping in and out of consciousness; and although the experience of consciousness is short-lived, you are working towards a wakeful state. Many Be-ings are unable to connect to the Spiritual Body because they are completely focused in the Ego Body and the Ego blocks the Spirit; yet they are getting glimpses of their Higher vibration through the spiritual work that is now taking place on the Earth Plane. Until you learn to align all of your bodies, you will only receive glimpses of the Spiritual Body, so the goal is to see yourself as a whole in alignment with all of your bodies.

Q. If we were able to enter the Astral Plane, would that ability, enable us to enter the Spiritual Plane and how would that effect the Physical Plane?

You would connect more to the moment in the Physical Plane. You are always connected to the Spiritual Plane regardless of any abilities to enter the Astral Plane. You have your lifeline to the Spiritual Plane. It is the umbilical cord to the Physical Body. However, you are not aware of this connection only because of the Ego Body's interference with the Mental Body. You are blocked from using the wisdom, knowledge and power of your Spiritual Body for your focus is trapped within the Ego's perception. It is important that you remember who you are, in Truth. In order to regain your memory you must connect to your Spiritual Body. You are drawing knowledge through all of your bodies, for all of your bodies, except the Physical Body, are Heavenly bodies. The Physical Body is a reflection of God through its uniting with the Heavenly Bodies. This means the Spiritual energy is present within the Emotional Body, the Mental Body, the Astral Body, and the Ether Body. Spiritual energy is blocked from these bodies by the perception of the Ego Body, although the Ego Body is also a heavenly Body, in its misalignment it blocks Spirit from the Physical Body. The Ego Perception creates the obstacles that cause separation from your Higher- consciousness.

In order to live within your Spiritual Body while in your physical embodiment....you must first discover the Truth about yourself. Only by discovering the hidden feelings within the emotional experiences of your Child-self.... can you hope to discover your True-self. The child within your Be-ING created the illusion, `the false self`.... and until you heal the child within....you will not recognize that you are...............

`Spiritual Eternal Energy`

CHAPTER IV
EXPLORING YOUR INNER WORLD

ASTRA Speaks….

*Who is <u>more</u> valuable and <u>more</u> interesting than you? Who could you desire to know so completely, to understand so deeply, rather than yourself? When you can answer these questions correctly you will see the truth about the power of who you are.

The `Inner-world` is where your True nature resides. All that you believe and follow in your Outer world that is hurtful or negative comes through your Child-self, the child lives within. The child within your Inner-world holds your fears and negativity. Also in your Inner-world your child shares space with your God-self…. that is all that is positive in your Be-ING. Your True self is hidden within your Inner-world and you were born to discover it. Discovery of your Whole self is vital for your ability to create a happy, peaceful, and productive life. We have said over and over again all that exists, exists from within. `Self-exploration` is the path to `Self-liberation.` As the explorers of your Inner-world you will always find more and more to discover, and your discoveries will set you free to live within your `True nature` as God Be-ings on the Earth Plane.

What you are in truth is `Spiritual Eternal Energy,` and the more you explore your Inner-world the more you will recognize this truth. What you experience in your outer world now is what you <u>hold</u> as your truth in your Inner-world. We do not say that all that you hold is negative for the Inner-child also <u>holds</u> positive feelings which reflect back to you through your manifested reality. The negative self, (which seeks always to hide from your consciousness) is what needs to be discovered and brought into the light where it can then be healed.

Once you learn to embrace your Whole self (the dark and the Light) you will transform your experience of the world in which you now live. Then the love that you are in Truth will reflect back to you in all your experiences.... and you will no longer be dependent on the darkness, the fear, and the negative emotions of the past. At this time you are in deep confusion and in order to clear the confusion....you must submit to the journey of your <u>false</u> identity; where you can experience the untruths that exist through your `Ego self.` Then you will begin to release the untruths and embrace what remains, your True self (God-self). On this journey you will discover all the demons that exist within your Ego-consciousness. When you are open to receive the guidance that self- exploration brings....all the insecurities, all the desire for destructive behavior, all the anger that creates <u>false</u> emotion through your Ego-consciousness will then be dissolved.

You have lived many lifetimes and through these embodiments you have been deeply affected by a <u>false</u> Ego-consciousness. In this Ego-consciousness you have created many `negative realities` therefore, you are in this trapped and confused position where you can identify the negative in someone else while never being able to see it in yourself. This is because your own negative attitudes and behaviors are so deeply buried. Therefore, when you recognize the darkness in someone else you believe it has nothing to do with you; that it is someone or something else that is blocking your freedom, your peace-happiness and creating your pain.

At this time you are having many experiences that are blocking your way for there is much concern, fear, and discomfort around relationships, meaning: that there is much discomfort around your relationship with yourself. It is time to have a True relationship with yourself and the only way to accomplish this is by discovering your `True self` through self-exploration. You identify with your false self in order to transcend it, in truth. Therefore, do not fear to go within and identify your darkness….and do not judge it, do not have guilt, nor do not punish yourself, rather learn to love yourself in spite of your darkness; knowing that the darkness is your false self and has been created out of the Ego's fear (Inner-child).

Forgiving the self comes when you bless and release through gaining complete understanding of the child within your Be-ING. The Child-self is the `Ego` now manifesting from without. Your Child-self reflects back to you through your outer world….showing you your fears, your anger, frustration, and lack of self-love. All destructive behavior your Ego can easily identify in others but yet, again, not in itself. See how hiding from the negative you hold within blocks you from living your `Best self` undefended? Here lies the reason why Be-ings blame all that happens to them on circumstances and other people, while never taking responsibility for their own darkness. It is impossible to take self-responsibility if you do not see your own darkness. You must first claim your darkness and embrace it, before you can transcend your darkness.

What does this mean? It is important to let go of the need to confront the darkness that you see manifested from without and rather, instead, confront the darkness that you hold from within. The need to concentrate on the ills of others is a destructive act; it makes it impossible to fight the darkness in you. Your desire to confront anothers' darkness perpetuates the darkness and it becomes stronger and more all-consuming within your own Be-ING. Within this approach you are blocking your ability to create more peace and joy. Within your own life you block your ability to love and to be loved. Therefore, to overcome the need to confront the darkness from without (in order to hide from your own darkness), you must seek out your own darkness and discover your own negativity, and all of the destructive attitudes that are buried in the depth of your Be- ING.

This may be hard for your Ego to understand because your Ego only believes in what it can see, touch, and physically identify with. What we speak of is not seen but felt; it is the physics which deal with energy and motion....through your unseen reality....your (Inner-world). Meaning: the Inner-child's perception through its feeling self is what blocks movement towards Truth in your Outer world.

We will now speak of how to make the journey into your Inner-world. Begin by asking yourself the questions that need to be answered in the moment. What is meant here is: that as you see yourself become frustrated or angry, ask yourself this question.

What is this feeling and where is it coming from? You might think that the answer is simple and that it is coming from what is happening in the moment, meaning: that something or someone triggered your anger or frustration. Although that may be true to your `Ego self` it is not true to your Inner-child….for it is the Inner-child that is experiencing feelings from the past and then transferring these feelings to what is existing in the moment. Now consciously (in the moment) you believe that it is an assault on your Be-ING that is taking place and you become angry at the darkness you see in someone else. Through this focus you have made yourself the judge and jury; blaming and condemning the other person, or situation, for your anger and frustration. The more you hide from yourself, the more you frustrate yourself, you deprive yourself of all that is good within you. Therefore, it is true that you must accept all that you are in order to dissolve all that you are not.

The child that you were is still present in your moment because existing in your DNA is cellular memory held within the cells of your body….and these memories live and affect your present reality. Awareness of the child's emotional structure is crucial for your understanding of your present adult emotions. Why is this so? Here in your Inner-world, in your Child-self, exists a world unto itself which is totally disconnected from your adult self. This is why many times you feel disconnected from your feelings and emotions. Whether your emotions are dark or light, they are not always recognizable, meaning: you are receiving signals through your cellular memory which create certain responses to events in your life that either alienate you from others, or create your intentions to be misunderstood and thus rejected. This happens because you are not aware that you are responding from a past cellular memory held within your Inner-world and, therefore, you are not truly responding to what is happening in the moment. Here you can see how the <u>child</u> is holding onto the past; overriding your positive intentions by clouding your vision of what is <u>truly</u> taking place in the moment.

The child felt deeply as it grew in this embodiment; it felt pain, joy, loneliness and separation from the Light from which it came. Understand the power that the Child-self holds in its feeling intelligence....feelings are what motivate every action and reaction in your life....and if you are not connected to yourself on every level of your Be-ING you will not be able to live a conscious existence; instead you will be in and out of consciousness and will pay the highest consequence for your ignorance of `Self.`

`Know thy self!` You were not born negative; your negativity was created through your Ego which is but a shadow of your True self. All the experiences that hurt and confused the Child-self created all the negative emotions and attitudes that now exist in your personality. Heal the child within and you will be free of your negative emotions, negative feelings, negative attitudes and reactions. Freedom through consciousness will then motivate your life and you will explore your `True self` <u>undefended.</u>

`I love myself when I am myself`.......

CHAPTER V
YOU AND YOUR PERCEPTION

ASTRA speaks ....

*You have been given a description of yourself as energy, and that energy has been broken down into seven bodies of energy in order for your consciousness (which is now within your Ego perception), to understand your energy patterns and how your Mental Body distributes the energy. To assist you in grounding the teachings through your Ego Body, we must begin to speak on the motivations of the Ego and how fragile the Ego is, in truth. You are all under the belief that your Egos are powerful and although they are, they are also easily threatened by their own reflection, meaning the Ego is `afraid of its own shadow`- the darkness within, in truth....for when another Ego confronts it, it is easily damaged by the influence of the Ego from outside (its own reflection).

Remember how we spoke of you as energy and how the manifestations created out of your energy were reflections of the perceptions you hold within your Ego? The Ego reflects fear, greed, anger, pain, in all of the experiences it encounters in the Earth Plane. It manifests, in truth, as a weak energy hiding behind the mask of strength and power through its ability to manipulate itself and its reflections (others) for, in truth, you either damage your own energy or create it Whole. You are the Center and, therefore, everything that manifests outside of your Center is a reflection of your beliefs….you draw in from without the experiences of your beliefs, of your perception.

This has been given to you in many forms through descriptions of the seven bodies, the child self, so you are aware of what has just been said. What is needed now is for you to begin to earnestly work along with these teachings which shall guide you on working to balance your perception in order to come into the Light of your true power as the Creator of your life.

To recognize who you are, you must begin to put yourself back together….just as in your nursery rhyme when "Humpty Dumpty" fell and all the pieces were scattered and there was a need to put the pieces back together in order to recreate the energy, you also are scattered in your energy….you are needing to put yourself together, and first you must begin to see and understand each Body of energy that you are in order to see yourself as a God-manifested Be-ING. Although in your rhyme no one could put the pieces back together because they were delicate and fragile in their structure (a clear manifestation of illusion), you, in Truth, are not fragile…. for you are made up of seven bodies of energy which can be united to create your Wholeness.

As it is, you do not recognize through your Ego Body that you are a God-manifested Be-ING, that you are a reflection of God-manifested in physical form within this Earth Plane. For this Body is within the illusion that all that exists is of physical matter and if it cannot be touched, seen, and sensed through all of your senses within the physical, it does not exist. This belief has penetrated all of your bodies, for your Ego Body interferes and manipulates your Emotional Body, your Mental Body, it blocks out your Spiritual Body, and it does not acknowledge your Ether Body nor your Astral Body; it only gives minor acknowledgment to the Astral Body through its attachment to dreams, and it is not aware of the significance of these dreams. What has just been given to you describes your sleep-state as a physical Be-ING within the Earth Plane. You are unaware of your Wholeness because of your attachment to the Physical Body.

In order to awaken (to become aware), you must begin to relearn about your own energy…. to rediscover your mind, your emotions, your Spirit and your Physical Body. The work is to come into the God-mind, for you are blocking your Higher-consciousness through your attachment to the Ego's beliefs. You are limiting your energy to one time, one body, one place of existence, which is this lifetime. This is a great limitation. It is likened to being on a desert island without any communication from the outside world, without any contact to other human beings. Without the knowledge of who you are, in Truth, you are asleep.

You must begin to acknowledge that there is more to who you are than you see, than you believe at this moment in your development. In order to recognize each of your bodies as a Heavenly Body connected to the One (the Creator), you must begin to accept that you have unlimited experiences within the Mind of God, that you have and you shall manifest yourself, your energy, into multitudes of expressions of the One. You are being told that you are needing to come out of a mind-set which tells you that you have lived only this life and no other, and to see that you are limited within this belief, and, therefore, fall victim to what you experience in this life. You are to release this illusion and see that you have lived multitudes of lifetimes within the Physical Plane, itself, that you have experienced God within the Plane of Spirit, that you hold all the wisdom and knowledge of the One because you are the reflection in Physical Body of the One, of God. Therefore, you are God, reflecting your energy into the Earth Plane.

Your memory of this Truth has been blocked by the Ego Body, the fallen Angel, the-Lucifer, of your Be-ING....and you must begin to accept the responsibility to break through the illusion and come back into your God-consciousness. This shall be done by re-teaching the Ego part of your Be-ING, by gently guiding the fearful child (Ego) into trusting in the love that created it. As we described the perception held by the Ego and how it distorts each of your bodies, we have also described the pure function of each Body through your God-self so you may begin to open your memory, broader and broader, of who you are....you may then take back the power from your Ego Body, your Ego-consciousness, and walk once more in the Light.

Before we go on, you must make a choice....for those who desire to come into the Light and be (in One) with the God Energy, the choice is to follow the Truth and to practice it in your physical world. This is not a simple choice for your Ego. It is difficult because it may separate you from many of the Be-ings in your life, if not physically, then spiritually and emotionally your perceptions may be at opposite ends. It will separate you from the past and leave you empty to receive the future. It takes a soul of dedication and deep love for the Creator and for all that exists within the Creation to make this decision. Once it is made, you are on a new path and you shall experience great resistance from your Ego which will fight you `tooth and nail`....for its only desire is to remain in control by continuing to hide from the Truth that it is One with God.

ANNA Speaks....

It was very difficult for everyone involved to be confronted with what seemed to be an ultimatum: either choose this path of work or be devoured by your Ego. Everyone, including myself, had great resistance, for no one likes to be told what to do. The Ego is too frightened of being controlled by someone or something to which it cannot physically connect. Here was ASTRA, unseen, telling us that it was time to choose: do we go on with the work or do we allow ourselves to decay in our Ego perception? I must laugh here--some choice! Anyone in their right mind, even in their right Ego mind, would choose the `path` rather than decay.

I see this as a loving manipulation of the Guardian Angel (ASTRA), who recognizes our Egos as frightened children, and is able to gently guide us into seeing enough truth to make the correct choice.

We have free choice within the Earth Plane, and ASTRA goes on to speak of the power of this gift, for we take this gift for granted. Many times you can catch yourself saying, `I have no choice,` `I am trapped,` `I lack money or power to change anything,` `I am a prisoner of my circumstances.` These beliefs exist because we have all been conditioned through the Ego not to believe in free choice. The Ego needs excuses for the negativity it creates....the gift of free choice removes the excuse which then makes our Ego feel as if it has lost control. We must come back to our God consciousness to recognize *that we have the gift of free choice and we never have to say `I am trapped,` I cannot change my situation,` `I have no choice.`*

Listen now to ASTRA to hear what was said on free choice.

CHAPTER VI
FREE CHOICE

ASTRA Speaks....

*What is the True meaning of this motivating term `free choice?` The Ego believes that this means to be free to judge and to act on that judgment. Judgment creates limitation; limited thoughts create limited action which is worlds away from God. When you are living in Truth you utilize your free choice to create unity, love and self- realization. You ask how is this done? The answer is: by understanding that you exist as One-energy, which you experience as positive and negative. Within your Mental Body you are of two powerful yet opposite perceptions, the God perception and the Ego perception. You cannot live between these two powers and be a powerful, creative force, for you are serving two gods which represent extreme opposite values, points of view and creativity. This conflict of thought which exists within blocks your Energy and creates negativity within the Earth Plane.

When an Ego is choosing it is choosing out of fear, for the Ego chooses through fear and judgment of self and others. This is because the Ego focuses on what is wrong and such a negative approach creates judgment....for in order to fix the wrong, one must first judge it as `wrong` and then replace it with that which the Ego sees as `right.` In this process many things take place. First, separation: separating from what is taking place in any given experience in order to protect yourself from your own judgment of being wrong; in other words, you create the judgment, and then fear that your creation will turn against you. Now you have created fear. Fear causes manipulation, dishonesty, secrets, desperation and pain. When you create out of Ego, your concern is to isolate yourself from being negatively affected by your own creations; therefore, you live in the illusion that you are separate from your creation and that you can survive its negative energy.

As a result, you weave a web in which you are caught and must constantly create entanglements with the negative forces which you now believe to be your reality but which, in truth, are illusion. You are limited in this reality, limited to the material struggle to survive your own darkness. You are in an internal combat with your demons of self- worthless-ness, loveless-ness, and greed….and this creates the decay that manifests on your Earth Plane, for you are being manipulated by your own manipulation. It affects you on every level of your life.

Example: You choose to be in the company of a family member who is negative and you make this choice only because you fear judgment of yourself from other family members should you choose otherwise. You, therefore, manipulate yourself through your Ego choice to protect a false God….the God of damnation. The illusion persists, for, in truth, this choice does not protect your energy; it creates what you fear most: damnation. Your choice to be with this Be-ING is coming from fear of judgment, not love; therefore, it is an illusion created by Ego to protect its false image of family unity.

Through your Ego you are sentencing yourself to extinction, for you are constantly putting out the fires of unity and love for your God-self.

The Ego's concept of `right` and `wrong` creates great separation from Truth, for the Ego continually focuses on what is right and what is wrong rather than what is truth. Truth is not measured by what is right or wrong; it stands on its own. It may appear that a certain action would be the wrong one to take in a given situation, but the outcome could prove to be a powerful lesson that creates new understanding for the whole of humanity. Example: the behavior towards your fellowman throughout the history of slavery in your world. This `wrong` act created by your Ego has been a powerful tool in awakening you to the truth which is that your Ego perception has created an illusion of your superiority over others and the threat of creating your own enslavement through these actions provide a powerful lesson. This truth is now alive and working to create freedom for all of humanity.

Only because of this awakening, not because of your judgments of right and wrong are you now beginning to grow out of your illusions that separate you from the wisdom you possess in your God-self.

When you choose through your God-self you choose to assume total responsibility for your own manifestations and their effect on the whole of Creation. Your mind is open to understand the entire design and meaning of life, of energy, seen and unseen. The unity of your energy (which holds your seven bodies of energy together and brings them into form and bestows upon them freedom of movement) is Love.

Love gives you permission to create, to breathe life into your creation, and to be free of judgment and fear....this is God.... this is who you are in Truth: God Manifested on the Earth Plane. You are this Unity, this Love, (The Creator). You are powerful and your power manifests through your free choice. Your choices create your reality your choices manifest your inner kingdom and your outer world.

First, you must understand that your inner kingdom <u>creates</u> your outer world. That which you feel and believe about yourself and, most importantly, how you love or lack love for yourself from within is how you will manifest your world from without; therefore, to choose through God's perception, you must see the God within and project that image into your world. How is this done? Through the Higher-consciousness you become conscious in every moment, in order to release the conditioning of your Ego Perception. To choose, you must be conscious, otherwise your choices are out of old habits instilled through fear and judgment. Working within the moment frees you to choose how you feel, what you desire, what is needed, and how it serves the Whole. When you are <u>not</u> conscious, for example, and someone criticizes your work, you respond through Ego by feeling hurt, angry, or rejected and you either defend your work or you feel to be a failure and abandon your work, or behave and respond in numerous self-abandoning ways. When you <u>are</u> conscious you are free to see yourself in truth as a God-manifested Be-ING and you can choose to listen to criticism about your work without being attached to the work and also to understand that disapproval of your work does not mean disapproval of you.

This attachment to your work is limiting....it creates in you limitation, for you become trapped by your creation of work rather than freed by it. Freedom is within the choice….when you choose to hear and you desire to create from your Highest vibration (intention), you are free to further create your work….you can be open to see what alterations or additions to your work are needed to make it serve its Highest purpose.

When one loves himself, he does not punish himself; rather, he truly nurtures himself by giving to himself what is needed in every moment. In this way he brings out the very best in himself, he brings out his God-self and bestows his love upon all that exists. Man and Woman serve through their greatest power: LOVE.

Through God Perception you acknowledge your power as the Creator of your own life and <u>you accept the responsibility for bringing yourself into the Light.</u> Once in the Light of Truth, you accept responsibility for changing your perception from Ego perception to God perception. There is only one union, in truth, and that is your union with God. All other unions are reflections of the One. So you see, if you choose through your God-self you manifest your `Highest` good; if you choose through your Ego-self you manifest your pain and decay.

Yes, it is that simple! Truth is simple only your Ego complicates it because your Ego needs to escape its own created fears, judgments, and punishments. Your God-self is at peace with what exists in the moment for it sees all the possible equations to every experience. This is because there is no fear to block insight and creativity. The Ego-self is like the child who is given a list of (`do's and don't's) in order to produce a certain result: obedience. This child will become fearful in his activities because he knows that he will be punished if he deviates from the rigid instructions in order to explore himself. So he begins, through his Ego, to find ways of exploring himself through lying and dodging responsibility. He is then on his way to weaving his web of decay.

In God Perception, the child is told clearly <u>through love</u> that he is responsible to himself. He is shown by example how to enjoy cooperating with others to accomplish something worthwhile. He is given permission to explore himself by encouragement through love and trust. This child will naturally do what is good for himself…. because he is allowed to be himself and is asked to take full responsibility for his actions. For example: he does something that causes him to get hurt, he is directed to examine why he got hurt and the different means he could have chosen to avoid getting hurt….also to accept the fact that he is hurt and to accept responsibility for taking better care of himself.

The word `responsibility` is the key to living in the Light. The Ego is always giving its power over to someone or something else, never taking full responsibility for the self. The path is clear: Free Choice + Responsibility = Love + Peace = Creativity (God). This takes place when you choose through your God-mind rather than your Ego-mind. First, you must begin to see the difference between the two minds, for you can choose only when you are aware that they both exist. Proof of knowing that you are in Ego-mind is when you avoid taking responsibility for your own creations and emotions and placing that responsibility on someone else or blaming it on circumstances and your lack of knowledge. So now with this awareness you are free to choose again, taking the responsibility back and bringing yourself into your God-mind (the Light).

CHAPTER VII
COMMON SENSE

My group was struggling with how to avoid the pitfalls in life. They were saying that maybe their lives were fated and that if they used the ability of free choice, how could they be sure fate wasn't really choosing for them.

So we asked ASTRA to teach us what we needed to understand about fate and free choice.

*Your fate: are the conclusions created by your choices in life which became your fate at the end of your journey, for you have through free choice created the outcome....therefore, your fate. Always remember you are the creator of your own life so your fate must manifest through you.

What you want to know is how you can create each moment so that you see the reasoning behind all of your choices. To find the reasoning you must activate the power of Common Sense, that which you have in common through your humanity; your ability to sense your surroundings and other people's soul vibrations, the common ability to smell, taste, feel, hear, and see.

Reading other people's energy (soul vibrations), does not mean that you are to become mystics, rather it means you are to become present in your life (conscious). Only through your presence can you come into contact with Common Sense. What is meant by Common Sense? While using the Universal Power of reason you can discern correctly why something happens the way it happens. Example: If you are reading a book that is telling you the world will end in 2012 because the Mayan Calendar shows how the ending is eminent and you believing this to be true begin to prepare for the end of your life. You then find yourself doing whatever you want or ever wanted to do, or say, to the people who have hurt you in the past.... even without proof of their intentions to destroy you (hurt you), you feel validated by what you have read and, therefore, motivated to speak your mind, recalling the emotional memories of the past. Now you have lost all connection to Common Sense....to the mutually shared energies that connect all of humanity.

In this act: you are motivated by the power of illusion. All Beings (through the Ego- consciousness) connect to emotional recall and without discerning ability; they fall into assumptions that sabotage their positive <u>creative</u> abilities. Your assumptions separate you from the `Higher` network within the human experience. Now you are as you would say," flying by the seat of your pants," where you land is at the edge of insanity.... <u>yes</u> that is correct, (insanity).

Clearly you do not stop and think deeply enough to see the truth which only can exist in the moment. The past is a memory driven by emotion and the future a dream that has not yet been created. Making choices based on none existing information in the moment, hanging onto the emotions of the past; can only manifest into your moment as something foreign (not based in present knowledge) and <u>cannot</u> reflect the <u>True</u> reality of the moment, therefore, creating your confusion and pain.

The Ego believes: there can be choice without consequence. When the Ego wants to experience through its senses it seldom weighs the possible consequences which are inevitable. Common Sense always organizes the mind to view outcomes possible within every choice made, therefore, prepares you to accept the outcome whether it is negative or positive. Your ability to take <u>responsibility</u> for your choices and actions in life must always remain active throughout the Mind, Body, and Spirit.

Yet, responsibility is challenged in the Earth Plane by man's belief in duality. Duality gives you permission to judge and to define truths versus untruths. This creates connecting to Common Sense, (common ground) difficult. `Duality` is a man made creation; which works to build the confusion within the mind and, therefore, serves as a great control device for those who would shape humanity in their own image. This statement may sound shocking to some and it may make sense to others. The man/woman who believes mostly in what is given to them and taught to them through others, would be shocked at this statement…. and the man/woman who thinks through all that is given and tests what is taught against the reality of his/her moment, sees the possibility of this statement being a true one.

What we are saying is an open mind holds only what exists in the moment leaving the space remaining to be filled with that which you have in common within humanity. **Common**

Sense serves the common ground on which you stand as a `Human- Being.`

This brings us to the concept of `One.` Because all is ` <u>One</u>` in truth, there could not be any separation that would create a lesser Be-ING. All choices would then serve the common thread you share as people who are living the gift of life bestowed upon you through the divine Common Sense of the Creator. Within this understanding you become present in your life; you are than able to choose what is best for you without fear of being different from others, therefore, you're able to raise yourself above false criticism....that which in the past would have activated the fears held within your Inner- child.

By living in the Truth while activating your Common Sense; you are truly the Creator of your own life fully taking responsibility for your choices, thereby manifesting the peace and joy which creates your love for self and others.

CHAPTER VIII
HONORING THE SELF

ASTRA Speaks….

*What does it mean to honor the Self? What self are we speaking of? Is it the personal self, Ego? Or is it the universal self, God? Maybe it is the physical self or the emotional self?

There is only One Self in Truth: God, therefore, we are speaking of honoring the God existing within the Ego body on the Earth plane. Recognize that all existence is a manifestation of God. Think of the self as a John Do or Mary Jane, who are the outer reflections of a deeper self; you are honoring the inner Be-ING and the outer reflection the whole self through your connecting to the love of the God within.

Honoring does not always refer to condoning everything you see and every feeling or action you take. Honoring means: remembering who you are from within your core. It is your attachment to the body and the senses which have seduced your mind and emotions into acts of negativity and greed.

Class member responds:

Q. Why then must I honor anything? Why can't I continue to embrace the experience of living my life with all my faults and loss of memory by staying in the moment (as you would say)?

Your moment (the ego's moment) is not staying in the moment in Truth. In this statement you are speaking of honoring your sleep-state by believing that you are in the moment when you are not. Think about what you have just said. Would you then honor your fears and your judgments, or the behavior that would hurt another? I think not!

Your ability to remember who you are in Truth sets you free from the Ego's illusion of self. It is by clearly understanding the deeper more `heavenly` qualities you naturally possess which will assist you in opening your mind more and more....creating your ability to <u>truly</u> value your own life. When nurturing these qualities you are honoring the Self, the God-self.

When one honors the self he does not abandon the self nor lies to him/herself or others in order to gain privilege over another. Example: The person, who feels jealousy in his or her heart is poisoned within the emotional body, and this poisoning comes from a deep lack of love for self. This lack of love motivates this energy to seek in others what he wishes for the self; while holding the belief that this will and can never be.... because he/she truly sees the self as being robbed and misused, misunderstood and abandoned by others. Anger consumes the mind and he begins competing with this person (that has possession of that which he or she has coveted for the self). Therefore, he begins tearing down the image of this Be-ING and in so doing; validates his/her own lack, by falsely placing the self above that which he false-heartedly believes is rightfully belonging to him or herself.

The energy of jealousy is the most dangerous <u>disease</u> a Be-ING can have, for it creates evil behavior and manifests destruction of self and others. The pain and destruction one does to another becomes ten times more damaging to the Be-ING who holds jealousy in his/her heart. When one holds this deeply negative energy, he is abandoning himself, leaving himself to face loneliness and pain…. for he cannot enjoy any gift that he or she has possession of. Can not look at the self and feel satisfied with what is seen….for one only sees lack and disadvantage, feeling deprived on every level of his/her Be-ING.

Understand what we say here: you cannot love the Self until you intimately embrace all that you are. Here lies the reasoning for investigating your whole Be-ING. By discovering the concept of `Oneness`….which exists within all of creation, you're discovering how to activate your highest intentions (motivations). While connecting to your heavenly qualities (Heavenly-bodies), you create your wholeness. Therefore, see how being in ignorance of Self creates your darkness…. for it is your Ego illusions that manifest your fear of not being good enough, smart enough, attractive enough or creative enough…. which manifests your jealousy creating your pain.

With this perception you think all that makes one powerful and happy in life belongs to others and not to you, you have nothing and you hold many reasons to confirm this false truth. One might be: that in your youth you were deprived and pushed aside, ignored, left on your own. Another could be: how you were never encouraged to see your gifts and how you received punishment which created the feeling that you were so deeply flawed…. and the people closest to you disliked you, or worse. All this would have created so much hurt and anger within the Child-self and would still exist now through jealousy, or in overt and hidden ways within your present adult self.

When moving forward in life the answer for grounding the Self lies in working to discover your gifts. Embracing all of the Self, (the dark and the light) by honoring all that you are and all the experiences you have lived up until this moment. Now in order to accomplish this – FIRST - you need to <u>heal</u> the anger that lives deep in your heart and soul. Through Self exploration you will heal the misguided perceptions of your Ego, (Child-self). Then you will come out of the darkness and into the Light of your True self, (God-self).

Now we shall continue by showing you how to open a clear path for discovering your Highest and Truest self. Follow closely the next chapter on the nine positive ingredients which all Be-ings possess through the `Higher-self.`

Chapter IX
The Nine Ingredients With-in Your True Nature

Anna's Thoughts

I will speak, at this point, on the impressions that I myself had as I listened to ASTRA speaking about love, trust and free choice. I realized that these <u>heavenly qualities</u> are the ingredients in man's true nature. I began then to visualize baking bread and I saw myself lining up the ingredients needed. As I saw myself blending the ingredients, I understood that what ASTRA said was very powerful, that is: we are given all the ingredients needed for us to connect to, to become one with, our Higher-self.

ASTRA will now speak to you about the ingredients within man's true nature, and this will become clear to you: Just as everything is One (for all things are connected), ingredients are the pieces of energy that make up the One (God). As all the ingredients in my visualization created the bread (and it is understood that without them there would be no bread), so it is that without the ingredients of our true nature, there is no connection to our Higher-self. We are not missing any of these ingredients in our Higher-self because they <u>are</u> our God-self. What <u>is</u> missing is the memory that we are God-manifested on the Earth Plane. As the bread nurtures our Be-ING when we ingest it, so does the memory of our God-self nurture us *through the realization and acceptance of the ingredients defined by the Guardian Angel (ASTRA). We are the bread, in truth, but we cannot nurture ourselves through our Ego perception because in that perception we are not conscious, we do not trust, we lack responsibility, we do not exercise our free choice, we cannot recognize truth, we are not aware of the love (the Creative Force) that exists within ourselves; and until we pursue these ingredients and experience them as who we are - we will remain in the darkness of our Ego-perceptions.*

How do we recall all of these ingredients and make them an active part in our consciousness of who we are? We have all been taught through our Ego-perception to place blame and responsibility on other people and circumstances and to judge and use those judgments to create our own truths and untruths. None of us have a true understanding of what these ingredients really mean, but we do understand one thing that `hits us right between the eyes,` (in our Egos): that we must relearn everything we believe we know, and release our Ego beliefs, judgments and lack of trust, so we may recreate ourselves. We feel great resistance from our Ego Bodies to this idea; nevertheless the desire for peace is so powerful that we continue to forge forward by asking ASTRA to define these ingredients for us. We have already received the first and most active ingredient, `Free Choice.`

SECOND INGREDIENT: LOVE (FORGIVENESS)

ASTRA speaks:

*We shall speak of the one ingredient that holds within it all of the other ingredients: LOVE....for that is who you are, in Truth. This is the ingredient that holds together all of your

Be-ING....this is the ingredient that creates all that exists in the physical world, in the mental world, in the emotional world, and the world of Spirit. The Power is LOVE. Because of your Ego perception you have blocked love from your consciousness. The Ego has distorted its true meaning and does not recognize the power, the creativity of this ingredient. The Ego manipulates the true meaning of love. Love is the greatest service that a Be-ING can enter into within his physical life, for it clearly brings him into consciousness and recognition of his Higher-self. There is a great deal to teach you about your perception of love, but first we shall speak of some of the ways that the Ego has distorted its perception of this ingredient, LOVE.

The Ego sees love as a weapon....a weapon of great power that the Ego uses in order to gain and hold control over others. The Ego barters with love, saying, `if I give you my love, you must give me respect, you must give me attention, you must give me your devotion, your obedience, your soul.` There are degrees, some as severe as just spoken, just described, and lesser degrees of how the Ego uses its power to control through love. The Ego does not see love as an unconditional giving. It views love as a prize, a commodity, a treasure of physical substance that it may own, possess, and control. You may believe that this is not truth: all the Ego is expecting, is love in return for the love given. What you do not recognize is that expectation distorts the love....for on any level of expecting a return for that which you give you are limiting your ability, your power to love and to be loved.

The Ego always sees love as something that comes from outside itself. It sees love as an energy that must be conquered--won, as a trophy is won for a sports event. That is why Ego Be-ings created the elaborate mating game, playing out the illusions of love, by dressing up in the paint and armor of a warrior going into battle....this is correct! Be-ings battle one another to win objects of love--to defeat one another in order to possess the trophy of love. The Ego creates each Be-ING as a trophy of love for itself. Even the love that you cherish for your children in the Earth Plane is selfish through the Ego's perception, for the Ego creates children in order to duplicate itself so it can ensure its continuance in the physical. Children are treated as possessions and they are molded into miniature replicas of the parent out of the greed of the Ego Energy. This is because man rears his children through the child within himself (Ego). That is why there is great confusion, pain, and resistance in the young children of the Earth Plane while they are working to grow into their true identity. They are so blocked with the identity of the parent that they, many of them, never make it to themselves. All of these crimes are committed through the perception of love within the Ego on your Earth Plane.

There are multitudes of crimes committed out of this perception that stretch out beyond the personal relationship into the relationship of country to country, the relationship of man to nature, the relationship between man and God because the distortion of the love energy blocks `trust,` the next most important ingredient in awakening to your God-self (Higher-self).

Love is what God is! The energy of love is the reflection of God within your Be-ING. You are, therefore, Love. This is difficult for you to follow through your Ego perception, so I shall give you a visualization of what is being said. You are of the (One) energy, which is God. Your Physical Body in the

Earth Plane is but a reflection of the One, as the light in your sky, called `star` is but a reflection of the planet from which the light that you see comes; therefore, in your reflection, your expression of the One is the energy of love. Love is the power that enables the physical manifestation to be. Love holds, binds, all the energy together to form substance of physical matter. Water represents the energy of love in that it holds all the elements of your plane within it. This is why your Physical Body is mostly made up of this fluid--water.

As you follow what is being said with your Mental Body, see how everything relates to everything else in the Creation. It is a continuous flow of energy coming from the One (God), and the Light of your Be-ING is within this flow--a loving reflection of the Creator. Until each Be-ING within the Earth Plane sees clearly that he is the energy of love, that he is an extension of the One, he shall not be able to free himself from the limitations of his narrow perception through his Ego Body. Before you can love another Be-ING, before you can love an idea, before you can love anything, before you can love God, you must first recognize the love for yourself....you must learn to love your own Be-ING unconditionally, for you cannot heal your Ego and the darkness it creates until you love it unconditionally. You must love every part of your Be-ING including the darkness, for only through love can you heal.... love is the healer! The power of love is immeasurable. It takes great patience, patience with yourself, with your Ego....and this can only manifest out of the energy of love.

What does it mean to love your-self? To love yourself, you must first understand yourself, you must see yourself as energy, you must see yourself as a reflection of God, and you must learn to forgive your Be-ING for its weakness, its Ego perceptions of greed, judgment, and fear....for patience and forgiveness are acts that manifest out of love. The work of changing your perception and your understanding of energy is not as over-whelming as your Ego tries to impress upon your Be-ING that it is. This tactic is what keeps you in an unconscious state, for whatever seems over-whelming creates a sleep- state within your Be-ING. In truth, all of these changes can take place <u>within the moment</u> of Consciousness.

The following questions pertaining to the ingredient, Love, were asked in Group: Q. How do our emotions tie in with the Love Energy?

The emotions are a tool that is used to experience the physical and to teach the lessons needed for your soul development. When you experience emotions from a High Vibration (your God-self), they are viewed in a bright and open manner. When you experience them in a negative vibration through Ego-consciousness, you view them in darkness (in sleep-state) so you cannot gain the knowledge hidden within the emotion. The emotions teach only when you are open to receive through your `Higher` consciousness.

When your emotions are teaching you, it is as if a prophet were telling of his parables (his stories) with which to teach. As they are not obvious in the telling and need to be examined in order to receive the wisdom within them, so it is with your emotions. It is not on the surface of the emotion where the teaching is....the teaching is hidden within and in order for it to be discovered (for you to gain the wisdom within the emotion) you are needing to be open in your Love Energy....

for only love can guide you to the wisdom that is within your Emotional Body. It is the love for yourself that opens you to receive the teachings that are hidden deeply within your Be-ING. All that exists is from within....to access the wisdom you must love yourself.

Q. How does love create energy? How does love manifest this energy into a reality?

Love is the constant energy force: it is God, it is the God Energy! It is not created by anything outside of itself. It comes from where all creation manifests and it manifests into the world you know through its own desire....it is because the Love Energy is so powerful that the desire to be creates its manifestation. That is the purpose it holds....to continue to penetrate everything that exists and be `One` with its Creation, for all that exists is the Love Energy. That is why God manifests in many shapes, substances, and penetrates your Be-ING, for you are a Love Creation--you are love manifested.

Q. Does this mean that the Ego is created out of love?

The Ego is also part of the same Energy. The Ego, in truth, is Love, as <u>all</u> is Love. It is because you, as a God-manifestation on the Earth Plane, have disconnected from this Love through the Ego part of your Be-ING, which fell into sleep-state.... once asleep you disconnected from the One. This is what created illusion and negative perception through the Ego. The Ego created separation from God - (Love) through its loss of memory and is left with the idea of `separateness` unto itself.

Q. How do we align our Egos with Love?

You must be within positive Love Energy to align the Ego. If you were to be within negative energy, you would only serve to strengthen the Ego, for it survives on negativity, illusion and separateness. Your Ego is always seeking to be separate from something or someone in order for it to feel safe and unique....and if you continue in this behavior in your Spiritual work you will only achieve in creating a more arrogant, a more illusionary- Ego. Because Ego is created out of Love it can only be aligned through Love (its true substance). That is why you must teach your Ego to `let go` of the illusions that block it from its true identity (Love). Your Egos are filled with fear because they are not connecting to the Whole. It is as if a soldier were in a dugout trembling with fear, that he does not permit himself to look out over the top to see that the war has ended and he is free to leave--his fear keeps him in isolation. This is as it is with the Ego it is within its own isolation, out of fear of being destroyed by what it has separated itself from: God (Love).

Q. When you told us how the Ego creates love versus God's creating love, what did you mean?

When the Ego creates something that is desired by it, it means that it is creating a pacifier, a thing of reward, that it needs to fill itself and to feel more powerful. For example: A man wants to marry the most beautiful and richest woman in the world. This is created out of Ego to build the Ego's image, so it is a pacifier and it will surely turn to negativity, for it is not love, in truth. When your God-self creates love it is an art, a sacrifice, a passion of great magnitude. It is always created to the good of everything that surrounds it. Love is a work of art....love from your true self is a masterpiece....love is God, the Creator....and you are love manifested through the Creator in the Earth Plane.

How is this so? It is the power of choice and perception that creates through you - you are the `Mani-fester` of your experience in the Whole of Creation and you are, in truth, powerful in love; therefore, you are God manifested. You are also experiencing the Ego perception; you manifest through this limited sight and your power is therefore, used to create negativity, and a false image of yourself - which separates you from God. This separation is what motivates you to divide your energy into small compartments of fear, fear of not holding your power, fear of extinction, fear of love, of giving, because giving becomes losing, losing to someone or something and this threatens your Ego's survival.

You are threatened because you perceive through loss, death and decay. This is the foundation for all your Ego perceptions. You hold on to the physical form like a frightened child holds on to a torn and soiled toy for fear of having nothing. You fear that losing the physical means complete extinction. This perception robs you of your true power, which is love. Love and fear cannot exist together. You cannot believe in both and be unlimited within your mind. You must consciously choose love over fear.

Q. I feel that I accept myself more, that I love myself; however, I feel blocks within my belief to go one step further and become the working actress that I was born to be.

You are learning to give to yourself through accepting your Be-ING; but this acceptance is at a level where you are recognizing the seeing of yourself in a negative light. You are beginning to see that negativity is your block, for when you see yourself as a person who is not capable of receiving work you are seeing yourself in a negative light....there is lack of love for yourself here. You are beginning to forgive yourself for this perception, and this is good. This forgiving is the first step. The forgiving is an act of love. Acceptance of where you are in this moment creates the space for loving yourself. In order for you to transcend that which you feel is negative about yourself, you must love that negativity. Meaning: Do not separate your dark from your light. It is important to understand that in order to heal you must love, so that which you see and judge as negative about yourself, you must accept and love in order to release the negative, knowing that you begin again in every moment.

You are recreating yourself when you are within love and acceptance. Your judgments of yourself hold you a prisoner to your Ego's perception and paralyze you from moving towards your goal.

Q. How do I begin to stop judging myself?

Judgment is what you must release. It is important for you to see this. I ask you, what are you judging? When you are judging your own Be-ING - in truth you are judging God - God cannot be judged for God is the perfection and the love that you are, in truth. Therefore, that which is negative and that which is positive are united in harmony, meaning: that which is negative in your perception and that which is positive, are both coming from the One, so you are in harmony when you can acknowledge and accept yourself as you are in the moment. As you are judging God, you are blocking yourself from creating because you are bringing in the judgment of the Ego vibration, allowing the Ego to block out the Truth, to block out the positive within yourself. As you are working.... that which you feel is negative in your work you must accept. You must begin to reverse the negative energy and bring it into a positive light. By shining your Light upon that which you see as negative, you will then transform it. When we speak of shining the Light, we speak of loving that part of your Be-ING that you are now judging. Only then will you be able to see the positive within, which will allow your creativity to rise above this illusion of imperfection. Example: As you go towards your career in the Physical Plane and you confront failure when not receiving a job, you must not see this failure as an ending. For, in truth, this failure is the beginning. How is this? Each time you fail you are one step closer to success, for each failure builds into a positive vibration for each time you pass through it and you get up and continue by not letting it stop you, you become stronger and more inventive, more creative in your approach, and this moves you closer to success. You are learning constantly through these failures, you are learning how to create balance between the positive and negative parts of your own Be-ING.

Q. I find as my Heart Chakra is opening there is a lot more self-esteem and self-love, but I am also finding the greatest lesson that I have ever learned is that I don't have to search outside myself for validation and/or love, that I am able to give these things to myself.

This is the greatest gift that one can give to oneself....to know your Wholeness and that you are not needing from without. It is important that all Be-ings learn this lesson, for you <u>are</u> Whole, you <u>are</u> One with God! As you go through your life and you become more connected to your Higher-self, you grow more patient, more accepting, and more open to what you need...and how to express your `True-self.` In other words, you are then content with your Be-ING....contentment is something that comes from within, and your outer world is a reflection of what you hold within your Be-ING. People in your life are manifested through the contentment or discontentment you hold for yourself. It is important that you begin to see this clearly: nothing outside of you can disturb the peace as long as the peace is held from within. You can be in a threatening storm and you can feel as if you were within its `eye` where there is complete peace and calm. Why? Because you are not relying upon the physical to give to you that which you already possess from your God-self. When you do not search for that which you already possess, then you manifest the beauty you already know. You will manifest the peace and contentment into the physical when you, yourself, have deeply connected to it from within.

Everyone on the Earth Plane is here to learn how to connect to the God from within. Even though the Ego blocks this wisdom, you are all learning through your experiences how to find your way back to your True self. Through Love you shall make your discovery. Ask yourself each day what it is that you need, what it is that you desire, in Truth....and the answer shall come in the unfolding of your life. Do not accept any obstacles. Know that they are an illusion, for they do not exist, in truth. Only the Ego sees them, for the Ego has created the illusion. Your God-self knows they do not exist. When you come across something that feels to be a block, you are to say, `there is nothing here blocking me, I will pass through this moment with love and I will find the direction to take.` When you are manifesting in the physical and create an obstacle, remember: each time this illusion tells you that you have failed, let the love from within you dissolve this idea and create a clear path for your energy to manifest your deepest desire.

Q. When you speak of obstacles, are you including physical obstacles, that we confront in everyday life which block us from obtaining a desired goal, for example, I am blocked from buying a building lot because the owners are in conflict with each other.

We are speaking of physical blocks as well as emotional, mental, and spiritual blocks that are within the perception of your Ego-self, for the Ego creates the blocks and is then limited by its creation; there are blocks that the Ego creates which awaken your Be-ING and strengthen your connection to your God-self, as well. You are also subjected to other Be-ings' creations of blockages. As in your situation, the Emotional bodies of these Be-ings are creating blocks to their releasing this property, and you are free to choose through your Ego either to be paralyzed by this manifestation from without or to choose to follow your God-consciousness and erase the illusion from your Mental Body, knowing, in truth, that there is no block here….for if this property is not to come to you, it is only because there is something greater manifesting within the Light for you to receive.

All blockages out of the Ego perception only serve to create limitation and fear; and when the pain that is created out of these limitations and fear is great enough, the opportunity to awaken to your God-consciousness is at hand….so obstacles, although they are illusions, are also filled with Light, for within them is a hidden truth that you have a choice to follow your fears into the darkness or call on your God-self to clear away the illusions, for they serve only to separate you from your True Power. You are the Creator and your ability to create is only as great as your ability to release the illusions of your Ego-self.

Many Be-ings are blocked mostly through the Emotional Body, for they have images in the Emotional Body of themselves as being abandoned, unloved, and lacking, and, therefore, fearful of obtaining what they deeply desire....for how can they obtain their desires when they are not worthy of receiving love. This Ego perception is what creates anger, destruction, and abandonment of self within your Plane. This is why it is most important that Be-ings of this Plane begin to see obstacles as they are, in truth: created Illusions of Ego perception. You are to always address each obstacle you recognize in a manner by which to discover how your energy can overcome this illusion and ultimately create what is needed to obtain the goal.

Sometimes there are obstacles that stop you such as sickness within the body. These are created out of your Higher-self, (God-consciousness) in order for you to learn a greater lesson for your Spiritual growth, for your illness is designed to save you from complete consumption by your Ego. Therefore, you may live with this obstacle for a long period of time or for the remainder of your physical life. You will learn more when you begin to add the ingredient of acceptance into your Be-ING. That is why all of the ingredients that you possess must begin to work within your consciousness, within your experience of this Plane.

Q. How does forgiveness create a stronger connection to love?

All acts of love increase the energy. Forgiveness is an act created out of love, for it speaks of letting go. In order to be within the love energy, you must learn to let go of that which blocks the love that is within each moment. Be-ings of the Earth Plane hold energy- feelings and emotions that are created out of the Ego perception; therefore, the holding blocks love. Forgiveness is an act of letting go of the negativity. It creates space and the space it creates allows love to manifest within the moment.

When a Be-ING forgives another, he is, in truth, forgiving of himself, for there is no thought, no act that another can perform against you that you, yourself, have not created out of your own energy. This is meaning, if a Be-ING performs a negative act against your energy, it is only there in manifestation because you have received it, accepted it, and called it to you. This is difficult for your Ego energy to understand and that is the reason why you hold and do not let go of `self- anger.` You are to begin to see that you must first forgive yourself for your anger and your separation from God in order to heal and to be generous in your forgiveness of others. As you have been told, everything is created out of your energy. You are the Creator of your life….how you are seen by others is that, which reflects what you truly believe about yourself. When you can see the Love that you are, in truth, you will be free of your negativity and you will create, through the act of forgiveness, more Light in your world.

ANNA'S THOUGHTS: LOVE INGREDIENT

ASTRA is telling us that love, as we know it, is not love at all, but a tool, a weapon, a means used to satisfy our greed! Let's think about that--through greed, we turn love into "profit" just as we turn money into profit. We believe that love works only if we "profit" from it in some way. That's our belief through the Ego perception. Isn't that an eye-opener? For example, we may seek to "profit" from love simply in the assurance it gives us that a "body" will always be nearby. Many people fear being alone so much that any "body" will do, with no love required, no emotional commitment expected, only the "profit" of not having to live alone.

You've heard the expression, "crazy in love." ("Crazy"- If you're crazy can you be in love? I'd say that is doubtful.) ASTRA speaks about the elaborate mating game and we are shown that the "mad about you" illusion is focused on the physical, so we dress up in "war paint" and the "armor" of attitudes that entice, manipulate and, yes, seduce another in order to attain that feeling of the conqueror-the "high" (the "profit"). We are forever seeking this feeling for ourselves. Man participates in this game because of his lack of love for self. It is this lack of love that creates the need to appear as the most important, intelligent, handsome/beautiful, and on and on, in order to win that "trophy" (the love from another) where we hide from our pain (lack of self-love). This is a game that our Egos play. Unable to experience inner love, we focus on imagery. We are always chasing the image again (illusion of love). We are taught these images as young children, being guided by our parents to adopt their likes and dislikes. The parents' images become our images, and false values are established. What is the consequence of this?

Throughout life we direct our choices based on these false values, chasing the image and never recognizing love as our true reality. Then, one day our relationship seems to fall apart, "the thrill is gone," our partner seems to have lost his/her allure, and there is only disappointment and emptiness. We realize we had never known our partner at all, we had known only our image of the partner! We leave the relationship to seek the next love (illusion). We chase the image once again and in this behavior we continue to rob ourselves of love, joy and peace (true reality)! Does this sound familiar?

So, where does the reality of love begin? ASTRA tells us that it must manifest within the self, which is self- love. Time and again we are told that we must first love our own Be-ING unconditionally; that is, to have a love relationship with ourselves. Only then can we manifest our self- love into a love relationship from outside, one that reveals itself in subtle, peaceful words and deeds and in a quiet understanding between two people. Emotional support through faithful encouragement and an unconditional giving, without judgment or pressure to measure up to another's expectation, is the reflection of self- love manifested. When we accomplish this, we no longer need to rely on "war paint" and "armor." We need only to be ourselves and to bask in love "from within and from without," to use ASTRA'S phraseology. I Anna am hopeful that this teaching will serve many.

Third Ingredient: Trust

*What does it mean to trust? Be-ings on the Earth Plane trust only in what is proven over and over again to them from without. In other words, if it is proven to them that they can trust the word of their Father when he speaks, then they shall trust what he says. If he is not consistent and does not follow through in his word, there will be no trust in what he says. The Ego's energy directs what is trusted and what is not, for only through the Ego's perception and through the Ego's experience does it either trust or mistrust in people, in things, in outcomes, or in its expectations. It is because the

Ego relies upon that which manifests from without that it trusts very little in the manifested world, for its manifested world is filled with many obstacles and negative experiences of pain and separation. So, in truth, before you can trust in the Ego's world, you must come into your God-consciousness and trust yourself. You must learn to trust your own energy....to trust who you are, `a manifestation of God`....to trust in your power to create balance and peace....to trust in your ability to overcome obstruction and negative manifestations through Love of Self.

Trusting is difficult for you within your Ego world, so you must work to create trust in yourself in order to pass through this world that you have created out of your darkness (fear). Trusting sheds light upon this darkness. You are the tool that will penetrate, through your trust, all of the negativity within your world. How do you do this? By beginning at your Center, for you cannot change the world from without, you can only change the world from within....and when you focus on your God-self and you work with that Energy and trust that Energy, you will transform your Ego....and this will serve the whole of humanity.

Your Ego will tell you that changing yourself will do nothing, for you are a small insignificant Be-ING in the total picture. But this is an illusion, an untruth, for as every Be- ING focuses on himself and focuses on recreating for himself peace, joy and balance within himself, that chain of energy connects one Be-ING to the next - and before you know what takes place, the world changes. Trust becomes part of the life for the Whole, and within your world you will visually see and experience balance and peace, for this explosion of power through trust will change and transform all of your institutions, your legal system, and your relationships with other countries, with your neighbor, your family and God.

Questions asked in group on Trust:

Q. Is trust something that comes naturally? Or do we have to learn how to trust?

You, as God Be-ings, are in the vibration of trust, it is your Ego-mind (perception) that is needing to learn how to trust; so, therefore, understand that your true nature is to trust and your illusion-nature is to mistrust and is in need of learning this trust. In this life, you are teaching your Ego to trust. The Ego has many blocks to trusting. Because it possesses great fear, it is limited in what it trusts. The work in this life is to come into your God-consciousness and align the Ego to your Higher-mind by bringing the Ego through all of the ingredients (such as love, trust, and so forth, with which it is familiar) to a peaceful space in which it can release its desire to control in order to survive it's fear of loss.

Q. When a person has had many failures in a specific area of his life, e.g., in relationships, wouldn't he naturally learn to mistrust his own judgments in that area?

He does mistrust his judgments and it is not a natural act, it is an act coming from fear, it is created out of holding onto the past. The Ego holds on to the past and brings it into the moment, and this habit of the Ego creates many obstacles in your life. As in this situation, when the Ego brings in the accumulation of experiences which are failures in relationships, it is creating fear in this area....and the fear becomes the obstacle that blocks trusting, for the fear works, in reality, to recreate the failures of the past. Why it does this is because it is holding the weight of the memories of what has come before, and under this weight it cannot release the fear of reliving the past....and it then works busily to recreate the failing relationship in order to quickly pass through the pain that it anticipates in the moment.

You must see how living outside of the moment burdens your Be-ING with negativity and fear, for how can you fear the present if the present is as it should be-an open space in which you are to create your life. As we spoke before of the canvas and the colors, you are the artist and the moment is your canvas. If the canvas is filled with the past or future, then there is no place to go, no space in the moment in which to create....your canvas must remain clean and ready to fill with the colors of the moment.

When you are in God-consciousness, no matter how many failed relationships of the past have been created, you are conscious only of the lessons learned through experiencing those relationships....and the lessons learned elevate your ability to create a lasting, loving relationship in the moment.

Q. When I have a close emotional attachment to another, I find it difficult to trust my own judgments and instincts in dealing with that person--it is much easier for me to trust my instincts in dealing with those with whom I am not emotionally attached. Why?

It is because you create separation through your Ego energy that this takes place....the Ego separates relationships.

There are relationships that it classifies as important and those that are unimportant. You must remember that your Ego always fears rejection and abandonment and it feels safe with whomever it is not familiar, for they cannot abandon or separate themselves in any way that is significant to the Ego's perception. This gives you freedom to be more trusting in your own actions towards these people. For instance, if you are dealing with a merchant and you feel you have been unfairly treated, you feel free to trust your instincts here and you feel free to act upon them....you do not take this merchant home with you....he is not constantly on your mind and this creates space for your energy to be trusting of yourself.

On the other hand when you are mistreated by a sibling, for example, you are immediately consumed with fear of abandonment and you question your instincts. You become stuck in a whirlpool of thoughts and emotions that keep you `spinning your wheels,` as you would say, for in this situation, the stakes are high....and because the Ego is in such fear of loss you constantly question what you see, what you feel, and what you know in the situation. You must begin to see more clearly that your Ego perception is that which limits you in creating peace, harmony, and joy in your life. If you cannot trust yourself, then you cannot trust any other Be-ING, for in order to trust that which manifests outside of yourself you must trust in your own `Power,` you must trust that you have created all manifestation out of your inner beliefs. Only then can you penetrate the illusions of the Earth Plane and change the beliefs that are not in Truth.

Q. What is the difference in my ability to trust that which is proven, such as the sunrise, the change of seasons, etc., and my ability to trust that which is not proven but taken for granted, such as being cared for by a parent as a child. How does trusting and taking for granted, relate to and differ from each other?

The universe and all within nature is `One` with your energy. You are connected to the sunrise, you are connected to the tides, you are connected to the seasons upon your Earth Plane.... for you are a creature that is nurtured and sustained in your very Be-ING by these elements, and, therefore, you are in tune with the movement of this energy. You say this energy is proven because it is consistent. Your Physical Be-ING is proven to exist because you, as well, are consistent in this energy as an element of the Earth Plane. You are born to and affected by this Plane as you affect the whole of the Earth. So in reality, this is the place in which you can trust without effort, for without your sun, for example, you would not exist, neither would the Earth, itself. Trusting here is at its purest form there is no mistrusting in your energy, because the mysteries of the Universe are far beyond the total grasp of your Ego, and will always be. Even your scientists will one day prove this Truth Themselves, and will acknowledge a Higher-Power.

When you speak of that which is taken for granted, you are speaking of the manifested Ego perception and how this energy within your Be-ING takes for granted behavior that is repeated. As you are growing in childhood, if your parents are responsible Be-ings, you will be confident that you shall be fed each day, sheltered from the world outside, the elements. You take this for granted through your Ego perception because the Ego becomes comfortable with anything that is repeated a number of times-- whether it is positive repeating or negative, it trusts, takes for granted, what is repeated....

that is the reason that when something has been repeated for a long period of time and it is negative, you become trapped by that negativity, for your Ego takes for granted that it will continue and so manifests its continuance. When this pattern is broken, the Ego also falls into fear for it is no longer on familiar ground, and it resists the new development until that development has been repeated enough times to create comfort in the Ego energy. This is why you must reinforce positive actions through repetition in order to assist your Ego in accepting the new perception.

You are creatures of habit, your Egos attach to habits, they block you from freedom of movement and creativity through attachment. The difference between trusting in Truth and merely taking for granted is that the taking for granted manifests through sleep-state (because the repeating creates sleep) and trusting comes from your God-self (wakeful-state)....for when you trust you are connecting to the Whole it is a natural movement of your energy, for you are trusting in the Creation when you are trusting your instincts, your feelings, your insights, your experiences within this Earth Plane.

Q. When a child experiences discouragement from parents or guardians in trusting his own abilities to explore and grow, how can he be expected to trust himself in adulthood?

He will not be able to trust himself in adulthood. That is why there are Be-ings of the Earth Plane who do not trust in their own instincts, decisions, and abilities....because these Be-ings, when young, are over-protected by the parent and, therefore, not permitted to experience themselves in their physical abilities or their abilities to make choices--the parent did all the choosing.

This is because Be-ings of the Earth Plane view their children as property and as miniature reproductions of themselves.... so they assume that the child has the same likes and dislikes as they do and the exact same limitations. What takes place here is that the children lose their own identity and take on the parents' identity. This is extremely dangerous to the well-being of a soul and many of these children are damaged emotionally and stunted in their growth. Of course there are those who overcome this stigma and conditioning, and break away from the images of childhood and create a connection to their True self.

This is why you are told that your Ego is the `child` within your Be-ING, for it is the fearful Ego/child that is limited in its perception because it holds the perception that is handed down to it through lifetime after lifetime and it is conditioned to create separation, loss, and decay. In order for this Ego/child to come into consciousness and experience its True nature, it must work for a wakeful-state, it must work to open itself to receive from the Creator by allowing the maturity of the God-consciousness (the adult) to enter and penetrate its perception and thereby release it from the fears that imprison its whole Be-ING within this Plane.

Q. Trust feels like a huge commitment, as if you were giving your power over to that which you are trusting; and this creates fear. Please speak to this issue.

The reason that you are fearful is that your Ego resists commitment to anything that it feels may create a negative image of itself. To trust your own instincts, your own wisdom, your own inner knowledge, is to release the control on your energy that is coming from without. In other words, your

Ego is accustomed and comfortable with being controlled by others and by familiar circumstances from without. To trust that which is taking place from within versus trusting that which takes place from without, you must align yourself to your God-consciousness....within that consciousness there is no fear of losing your power. The Ego fears losing a false power, it believes that it has to be on guard at all times in order to survive....and this belief prevents your Ego from trusting completely any situation or other Be-ING. It only trusts so long as it can control that which manifests.

Understand, therefore, that when you are in Truth (in your God-consciousness) your ability to trust raises your energy above the dense, limited, dark vibrations of the Earth Plane. It allows you to soar like an eagle above all negativity and fear that are held in the gravity of the Earth Plane. You do not have to be dense and heavy Be-ings because you are within Physical Body within the gravitational energy of the physical earth, for your energy goes beyond the physical.... and when you begin to understand that through your Mental Body when its connected to Spirit you can rise above the density and the limitations of your Ego perception, you will then be able to learn your lessons and create balance and become One with God.

ANNA'S THOUGHTS: TRUST INGREDIENT

ASTRA is saying that we cannot trust our outer world because it is filled with negative illusions. In order to survive these illusions we must first trust ourselves -"the buck stops here." I understand this to mean that when we are feeling paranoid about whatever is taking place around us, instead of letting ourselves get trapped *in the outer confusion we must go within and take inventory. Example: when someone inflicts either emotional or physical pain on us and it causes us to become fearful and confused, we then begin to believe that we <u>are</u> the fear and confusion. At the moment we feel we are sinking into this belief is the moment we need to go within and take inventory which will show us that we are <u>not</u> the fear or confusion. We recognize that we forever remain unchanged that we are a manifestation of God, a creative force in the universe, a loving vibration of Truth. This inner wisdom frees us to connect to our creativity, which, in turn, guides us to release all fear and confusion. Only when we trust this inner wisdom can we trust our ability to cope with whatever takes place in our outer world and can we know that we are <u>in</u> the world but not <u>of it</u>! We are able then to remain calm through each storm in life, we are able to accept life on its terms, we are able to be confident that Love will heal the misguided energy that creates pain and separation in our physical world. We are then able to heal ourselves and resurrect our life out of the darkness and into the Light!*

Fourth ingredient: Acceptance

*Acceptance is a very important part of your Be-ING that creates the path to peace from within, for in order to create peace you must accept that which is within the moment. Your Ego-consciousness has great difficulty in accepting its creation of fear. If a situation is negative and threatening to the Ego perception, it rejects it there is no acceptance, there is resistance….and resistance creates more fear and manifests behavior that creates karmic energy.

In order to be within God-consciousness (to experience peace and balance) you must be open to accept that which exists within the moment. You can only do this when you are conscious (aware) that you have created that which exists. When you are conscious of this truth, then you are free to accept; but if you, through your Ego, do not take responsibility for that which has manifested in your life, but rather give it to others and to circumstances from which you have detached any responsibility, you will not have peace, for there is no acceptance.

It is only a Be-ING who is focused within his God-consciousness who can see that he is the Creator of every moment in his life....so he accepts his responsibility for his creations, even those that are negative, for he understands that they were manifested in order to awaken him from a sleep-state, understanding that they came from his Ego perception, and that his True self (his God-self) was not the co-creator in his creation; therefore, through his God-consciousness, he is open to examine his creation and to pursue a balance.

Acceptance can be likened to a running stream. As the water runs down the mountain it is going with the flow of energy.... it is accepting its direction - it does not fight to stop and go in the opposite direction, it is open and, therefore, it receives the direction that unites it with a larger body of water. Again, you are the stream and your God-self is the larger body of water with which your energy is being directed to unite. So understand, when you accept that you are an extension, a reflection, of the One God then you are able to accept that this life in which you find your energy is but a small minute part of your True self....and that it is a vital part, in that, it experiences directly through the senses all of the Bodies that are within the <u>One</u> consciousness.

You experience not only through the Physical Body but you experience the mind of God, the creative power of God, the creative process, itself, in a very intimate way. It is all held within the perception of mind. Your True identity is hiding somewhere within your perception, within your mind, and you were born to discover it. Only through acceptance of what is in the moment can discovery occur, and connect you to the Power that you are, in Truth.

Questions asked on Acceptance:

Q. I am working on accepting myself, and I find it difficult because I have a sense of lack from within.

In order to love yourself you must accept everything about you. You have possessed glimpses of loving yourself only in particular situations that created a sense of peace for your Ego, and as soon as the situation changed and your Ego felt threatened, you fell out of love. It is as if you were another person. For a moment, think of yourself in that way. When you are with other Be-ings and they are behaving the way you like, you love them and accept them; yet as soon as they do something that does not suit you, you fall out of love with them in that moment....you become angry or disillusioned, you judge them, you feel threatened....and fear takes over and you doubt the relationship.

When you do this within your own Be-ING, you become the fickle lover of yourself. You only accept that which you feel is rewarding and safe for your Ego. You must begin to see how you do this with your own energy. You love and accept yourself when your Ego feels safe, when it feels that it will not be rejected, abandoned, or destroyed in any way. As soon as you challenge your Ego by doing something that threatens it in a Physical or Emotional plane, you fall out of favor with yourself and you judge your actions. In this way, you are not accepting of who you are….and by not accepting, you allow fear to consume your energy and block you from truly experiencing your life.

Q. You say if a Be-ings Ego does not accept the behavior of himself, he becomes a fickle lover. How then do you discern what is right for you? This confuses me because even though you may be accepting of yourself, you may still find that there will be others whose behavior you cannot accept.

When you are truly in acceptance of yourself with all your faults and your strengths, all your actions and reactions, this does not mean that you condone your negativity. It means you recognize it, that it exists, and you accept its existence….for only through accepting can you balance the negativity that you see. You do not deny it, you do not hide from it you do not try to manipulate others so they will overlook it. You are open and honest with all that exists. This is acceptance! Accepting does not mean condoning it does not mean that you become rigid or that you are casual in this acceptance. True compassion manifests from acceptance.

When you accept yourself, you are giving yourself permission to grow by allowing yourself to make mistakes and allowing yourself to feel your emotions and to express them, even if they are negative….by giving yourself this freedom, you are able to love your whole Be-ING, and this love creates the awareness that you are growing through your experiences in this life, that you are learning of your God-self in every moment.

When you can do this for yourself, then you can do this for others, as well....in accepting, you are permitting others to be who they are, where they are, in every moment. You do not judge them or reject them; you give them space in which to find their own way, for judging creates obstacles and confusion, and rejection creates pain and a deep sense of loss. At the same instant, this does not mean that you must embrace them and permit them to judge or reject you.... it does not mean that you must keep company with a Be-ING who is not vibrating at the same level of consciousness as yourself. What it does mean is that you love them as you know them in Truth, as an extension of God (a reflection of the One)....and you understand that where they are vibrating is exactly where they need to be in order for them to grow into their own awareness, for every Be- ING must experience the darkness in order to come into the Light. You must hold compassion within your heart for their journey as you hold compassion for your own, then you will be in true alignment with the ingredient `acceptance.`

Q. Does this mean that we don't have to like them, but we must love and accept them? Does this include ourselves; in other words, we do not have to like our faults but we must love and accept ourselves in spite of them?

You are speaking now of discrimination. Discrimination is a high vibration when it is used within the Light, for every Be-ING is comfortable and at peace when he is vibrating with like-minded Be-ings, meaning Be-ings who are at the same level of consciousness as himself....so in order to continue to create peace and balance, you discriminate by focusing your energy where it is free of Ego negativity. Therefore, if your energy is uncomfortable with `Rock` music, for example, and it feels more at peace and in tune with classical music, then you discriminate against the `Rock` music in order to give yourself that which you need to sustain the balance of the vibration in which you are. So you can accept people as they are, and discriminate in choosing who you want to spend time and energy with, according to what your energy needs to further your peace and balance.

You are working through your God-consciousness when you are aware of your whole Be-ING and its needs, its abilities and its mission in this life, for every Be-ING in the Earth Plane has a mission to accomplish within this incarnation.... and only if it is accomplished, will you raise your energy to the next level of existence. Through your discrimination you are protecting your energy from falling into past Ego behavior (meaning past-life behavior) and present-life behavior as well, for within these behaviors you are in sleep- state. In this way, through acceptance of who you are, in Truth, you are creating more love for the whole of mankind....so you are to see here: accepting that which exists in the moment within your own Be-ING or (anothers), is meaning to see the truth and acknowledge it, for when you can acknowledge truth you are free to choose a Higher Truth....this is what is meant by accepting with Love all that exists within the moment.

Q. I realize how I have grown; and reflecting on the person I was before I changed, I find it hard to accept that former `me.` I am no longer comfortable with those who knew me as I was before. Why?

You are looking back and that is why you are not comfortable. You are not letting go of that former person. Somewhere in your consciousness you continue to hold on to what was, and your Ego is continuously comparing the past with the present. That person no longer exists, for only that which is in the moment exists. When you are looking backwards, you are bringing in an energy which ignites and creates confusion in the present, for you are bringing to life the past, you are resurrecting the dead....this cannot be done, in truth, for the dead no longer exist.

See how you are crowding your space within this moment by living your past self and your present self at the same time. When you are with others who create for you the memory of what has passed because they treat you in old ways that no longer are in alignment with who you are now, you must continue to stay conscious of who you are by directing their energies to see you more clearly. This means you must speak to these Be-ings in an open and honest way in order to teach them of who you are now. Because the Ego is trapped by habits, people do not easily recognize a shift in someone else's way of being; and even when the Ego does recognize, it resists change and tries to use the same tools and information that it is familiar with to continue to deal in the same way with that person. That is why it is important to be steadfast in your new creation of yourself.

Your feelings of rejection from those close to you from your past are still very much alive within this moment, and these feelings of rejection have given your Be-ING the idea that you are not worthy of love, that you are not a worthy Be-ING.... for now you find yourself no longer accepted in the same way by the people who knew you as you once were....and this is what creates the deep feeling of rejection. What you need to understand here is that the acceptance cannot come from without....it must come from within. You are to accept yourself, you can only find peace and connect to the power within this new growth of your Be-ING by accepting who you are....for when you are focusing on receiving acceptance from others you are giving your power (your God-self) away, and this can only cause pain and separation from the God within.

Q. I have been exploring the acceptance of myself and acceptance of that which happens in the moment. You tell us to accept everything and to hold nothing. Sometimes thoughts come into my mind and I try to intellectualize them--then I catch myself and try to let them go. Am I on the right track?

This is the right track, for you are a Be-ING who is confident in his intellect and not in his emotions. You do not accept yourself on the Emotional Plane, and you are consciously working to accept that which you feel and to learn to release the desire of intellectualizing the reasons for your feelings, you do this through learning to accept the past experiences that created your feelings. As we have said before, when you accept, you bring the Ego into the Light....you do not burden yourself with creating reasons through the Mental Body for this acceptance....in accepting, you do not intellectualize, for if you do, you are telling yourself `I accept this only if I can figure out a reason to accept--I accept this only if I can make it what I believe it should be--I accept the situation only if I can manipulate what takes place.`

Your mind and your heart must be one, for your intellect can only create reasons for your actions....and when you are accepting, in Truth, you are focused in the moment and your energies are aligned with that which is taking place, so your whole Be-ING automatically accepts what is there. No intellectualizing needs to take place. You are in the moment and everything that is there is exactly as it should be (the past creates the present). The desire of the Ego to change the reality of the moment does not exist. If it does, then you are unconscious and you are creating conflict through the Ego-mind. Accepting is an acknowledgment of what is taking place in the moment. Change manifests through acceptance.

ANNA'S THOUGHTS: ACCEPTANCE INGREDIENT

*I believe it is expectations that block our ability to accept. Expectations are dangerous in that we believe them to be real, concrete, and already manifested exactly as we had planned them to be through our thought process; when we become conscious, however, we are graced to accept the truth that expectations are merely **illusions of desire**.*

Our expectations are powerful because we invest everything we are, everything we have, and everything we believe into them-- our energy, our hopes and dreams, everything we desire for ourselves. This clearly is the reason why we cannot accept the truth when it contradicts the expectation.

It isn't so much that we don't see the truth--it is more that because we invest so much in the expectation, that to then accept the contradictory truth, is much like death to us. Example: We marry and our expectations are that our spouse always will be faithful and loving. What does this mean? It means that we plan our life around these expectations, to live in complete confidence and comfort to plan the future, raising a family and growing old and retiring together. What happens when suddenly we learn that our spouse is unfaithful? We find that we cannot accept this simple truth! We suffer, due not only to the unfaithfulness but also because our expectations have been shattered. It is, again, our lack of love for self that blocks our ability to accept the truth. This causes us the greatest of pain.

Fifth Ingredient: Truth

*Within the Ego perception, there are many truths. The Ego creates truth that satisfies its expectations. In other words, if, within your Ego, believing something that makes you feel secure in the moment becomes your truth, it does not necessarily mean that it is true. Truth is an energy that has no longevity through the Ego perception, for what is true today may be a lie tomorrow-- it may be a lie in the next moment; so understand that through your Ego perception, you use the word `truth` when it suits you, when it fits your illusion.

Truth is simple in that when it is present it cannot be denied.... it is accepted by all who are exposed to it. In each Be-ING on this Earth Plane there is little connection to Truth, for, in truth, you do not see yourself as who you are and, therefore, you are seeing untruths about yourself. You believe things about your personality that are passed down to you through the perception of others, you believe that your faults are true and irreversible and you understand only what you can reason through your Ego-consciousness....and that is why every individual holds his own truth that is separate from another.

Here, again, you are dividing your energy--you are living a reality created out of the great illusion of separateness, for there is only One Truth and that truth is that all that exists is One, is God....and within this truth, you see clearly the truths within your own Be-ING; which are that you are responsible for your creations, for you are the Creator of your existence within this Earth Plane. You hold the power for raising the vibration of the Whole by seeing this One Truth within every Be-ING, within everything you do, within everything you create in this lifetime.

See clearly that Truth is eternal, it is never changing it remains constant. Only that which is constant can be true. All the shifts in your energy, all movements in the mind that continuously change your focus, are untruths, for this is the illusion playing out its many manifestations, and, therefore, there is no permanence in these truths....so they are illusions of mind! You do not have to look for Truth for it exists in the eternal energy of God....and to know that this is your identity is to know Truth!

Questions asked on Truth:

Q. Does knowing ourselves in Truth give us power?

By believing in the Ego's illusion of the Earth Plane, you have separated from Truth, in separating from Truth, you have separated from your power, separating from your power has created pain, negativity, and imprisons you to karmic lessons.

Your God-self does not claim the Ego's illusion; however, it accepts the manifestation of such illusions and remains constant in Truth (neutral), never being seduced by the Ego's creation, and, therefore, always free to create. It is all about the perception that you hold through your Ego-consciousness, for you hold many ideas about yourself and every one of them is false. Whatever you think about yourself is incorrect, for your Ego has created these ideas--the Ego operates through illusion and that is why Truth becomes illusive....and your Ego works to protect these false truths.

See the `Truth`: That you are all that exists....and do not claim any one part of your existence! This is meaning: do not claim your goodness--nor your `evilness`--nor your cleverness--nor your ability to create because in claiming what is created is separation....you then become what you claim and your energy is limited to that one part of your Wholeness, so you are no longer free to receive all that you are, which is God.

This is difficult for your Ego to understand, but if you claim <u>nothing</u> then you are free to be <u>everything</u> that exists within Creation....and as your energy moves, you are free to embrace every part of you as it manifests before you, for you are not obstructed by the illusion that you are any <u>one</u> thing, so you are in total freedom to accept that which exists in Truth, in every moment.

Life can be joyful if it is experienced through the awareness of your True self. If you take this journey in Truth, you will be free of pain and fear. To know truth is to know God!

Q. It is often said that hearing the truth is painful, and I believe that it is better not to always speak the truth in order to spare another person's pain.

This is the Ego's belief system: `spare the truth.` What are you sparing when you spare the truth? The answer is `nothing,` for you are replacing illusion for truth you are believing that you are protecting another from a painful truth....and this perception that truth is painful is what makes it painful, for pain is part of the Ego's experience that ultimately leads you to joy....without pain there can be no awakening, no realization of your God-self.

When you speak of truth that hurts another, in reality you are sharing truth that creates freedom for the other. The hurt comes from the Ego's resistance that is due to its fear of being freed from an untruth, which blocks it from growing into God-consciousness. The Ego fears God, which is why Be-ings are comfortable with what is familiar, because fear of God creates fear of change they do not trust that if they step into the darkness (fear), they will come into the Light of Truth. Only being connected to Truth can you come into the Light in any situation.

Deliberately keeping the truth from someone is giving them more pain because they remain in a lie and they continue to live in an illusion by believing this untruth. When you do this, it is as if you lock them in a dark room and they cannot find the door from which to get out. Speaking the truth is likened to turning on the light so they may see the path to the door....now they are released from an untruth, and the pain is an experience which they must pass through in order to find their joy, for joy does not come to you -- joy exists within you. The untruths that you hold hide your joy from you. When you find the courage to walk through the pain by accepting Truth, you shall be in your natural state, which is joy.

Q. You have said that Truth cannot be denied. Since learning the importance of Truth, I now feel that the responsibility to always speak what I feel to be the truth is burdensome.

The truth is important for it frees you from your Ego-consciousness. The saying that you have, `the truth shall set you free,` is within the Light, for only through Truth can you gain freedom - freedom from your pain from your negativity and your illusions. Within your Ego there is great resistance to seeing and to hearing the Truth, for the Ego prefers illusion because it fears Truth; therefore, only when you are within your God-consciousness can you face the responsibility of speaking the truth.

Understand this clearly: we have said before that because it is your truth does not mean it is truth. So, do not believe that whatever you feel to be the truth must be spoken. You are only responsible for speaking the truth about yourself you cannot speak about another only yourself. An example: Within a relationship, if you are aware that you are not being truthful to your partner, you must take the responsibility to become truthful, even if you are aware that doing so will create pain for your partner. Remember that speaking your truth will free you from the burden that you carry in the untruth that you have spoken. This means, you do not tell another person the truths they hold, for you cannot know this and you are not responsible for what another Be-ING holds within his consciousness. You can only take responsibility for yourself.

The burden that you speak of comes from your Ego's fear of facing the truth about your motivations and desires in any situation. To release this burden, you must value truth with all your heart. Only through the love energy can you create your ability to face your own truths.

Q. Why does the Ego fear Truth?

Your Ego fears Truth because it holds guilt for separating itself from God. What you need to understand here is that at your beginning you were in alignment with all of your Bodies and your Ego was aware of God. The Ego created separation when it became obsessed with the physical senses….so your Ego is the fallen Angel (the Lucifer) of your Be-ING….and Truth threatens its existence and guilt threatens its survival, for your Ego energy is the part of your Be-ING that is the child who has disobeyed the Father and fears the wrath of the Father for his behavior.

In order to understand this clearly, you must see through your God-consciousness how your Ego fears being caught, tried, and sentenced to death by God. The Ego does not see God as a loving energy, as part of itself - it sees only separation. To your Ego-self God is an entity that lives far above the physical world and holds judgment for everything that you do within this world. The Ego believes that it will pay severely for anything negative that it is caught at doing. This is why your Egos try to rationalize your negative behavior, for your Egos are always covering up the truth in order to stay hidden from God. The fear of Truth is powerful, for the Ego believes if it must confront God and also accept that it is God, then it must be destroyed because of its separation into the darkness. This means death for the Ego, and that is why every Be-ING on the Earth Plane, through his Ego-consciousness, fears his own death.

In order to release the fear of death, the Ego of every Be-ING must come into alignment with the Heavenly Bodies and take its rightful position while within the physical world....then fear will no longer exist within the mind of man and you will be free to create peace and balance and raise the vibration of this planet that you call `Earth.`

Q. Can you assist us in releasing our fears? I am especially afraid to say what I think to people with whom I work.

Most Be-ings are afraid that they shall be punished for speaking the truth, either they will lose their job, or a loved one, or their image, or even their life, itself. To assist you in this, first you must be patient with yourself you must not take on the perception that truth is something that should just be thrown at another without feeling, without love, for you must always work with the love energy and speak truth with love. For example: If you have a personal dislike for someone and you are judging them and you feel you are telling them what you think and assume to be the truth, this is not correct for you are burdening them with your belief system and this is not truth! It can be hurtful because, in reality, it creates more untruths.

Through your God-consciousness, you only take responsibility for telling the truth about yourself. Never tell people what you think only what you have discovered or what you feel. Example: When you are working with someone and something comes to pass where you discover the truth that you have been lied to, you must not fear speaking to this person about the lie, for if you do not confront the truth, you will be consciously permitting yourself to continue with the lie....and this decays your whole Be-ING, for you are conscious of this lie and you further create separation from your God-self by giving your power to the creator of the lie. You damn your whole Be-ING and deepen the hatred for yourself, and abandon the love, so, see how you create your life in Truth? How you are the Creator?

In every action you take, every time you look away, and every time you confront the truth you are creating your existence, your whole Be-ING. Consciousness is what you must possess in order to be aware of the energies, whether they are positive or negative, for only through consciousness can you create God's image.

The power of Truth is Eternal and death never consumes it. Your connection to Truth, your commitment to serving the truth, renders your Be-ING (Eternal). This is how you eternally continue in Creation, serving Truth (God).

ANNA'S THOUGHTS: TRUTH INGREDIENT

It is clear to me, in listening to ASTRA, that there is only one Truth (the Universal Truth, God) which is that we are God-manifested in physical form, that we are the creators of our own lives. The Ego, however, creates illusions of truth in its desire to hide from the Universal Truth. Why? Because the Ego, in its fear of judgment, separation and pain, causes us to believe in an illusionary truth which we expect will shield us from our fears. It might be something as simple as believing,` I am wealthy and, therefore, I can control my environment I can live in the most prestigious area where I am protected from crime, unwanted intruders and the blight of the world -- so I am safe.` This belief is an illusion, safety comes from within, not from without. Creating such a physical separation in order to protect one's self tends only to *deny one a full life. This gives a false sense of security wherein a chain reaction of one illusionary truth feeding into another occurs. Man escapes his responsibility for self and relies on these illusionary truths to protect him, to validate him and to ensure him a secure life, wherein the price he pays is a lack of consciousness of Universal Truth; consequently, he is manipulated by his false belief system of truth.*

When living within the Universal Truth, we are the creator of our own existence and protected from entrapment within the material world. We live our lives through love of Truth and we serve the Creation when working to serve ourselves. While we are living in Truth <u>all</u> is served.

*Living a life within Universal Truth is a life of emotional riches. There is a connection to all that exists through a powerful sense of SELF. This powerful sense of self enables us to create the ultimate freedom – **freedom from fear**.*

SIXTH INGREDIENT: CONSCIOUSNESS (AWARENESS)

*The Ego defines consciousness in this way: If you are walking, talking, and functioning in your work, the Ego believes you to be conscious. If you can communicate both what you need and your emotions in any given moment, the Ego believes that you are conscious. It believes you are unconscious when you are sleeping or when you have passed out, meaning you can no longer speak or stand erect.

In truth, these definitions do not draw a true description of consciousness, for you are only conscious when you are focusing all of your energy into the moment. What does this mean? Clearly, it means that you are free of thoughts and emotions of the past, that you are free of expectations and illusions of the future. Your Mental Body is as clear as the white canvas of the artist, and with this clear mind you are present to absorb the sounds, the colors, the vibrations, the emotions that exist within the moment, filling your canvas with the information of what is present, arming your energy with the knowledge and the wisdom of what exists. In this state you are the Creator, you are God, for you possess all the knowledge that is needed to create in that moment. You are aware of what is needed and you serve that need....for God is in service to his Creation and you are able to serve only when you are conscious, of this Truth.

The consciousness of the Ego is an illusion, for within your Ego perception you are in sleep-state. You can connect to this by comparing this state to `sleep walking.` When a Be-ING is sleep walking, he is erect, he is walking, he may even speak, have conversations....but he is not conscious. Therefore, you could not trust him to operate a vehicle, for example. Multitudes of Be-ings are being trusted with more than a vehicle in their unconscious states. This is why your Earth is in deep imbalance and is suffering....because it is being served by `sleep walkers.`

It is not difficult for you to examine how you operate in this state. You can do this by examining your interactions with intimate relationships, and you will clearly see how you bring the past into every confrontation, how you judge the partner when your expectations are not met, how you run away from your responsibilities because you feel rejection from another. All of this and more is a statement of your unconscious state.

Working to come into consciousness is continuous. You cannot take a vacation or a short break from this work. To be conscious, you must first be aware when you are unconscious. When you become aware that you are in sleep-state, it is your responsibility to come into consciousness (to participate in the moment), for only within the moment can anything take place; so within the moment you are to release what is blocking your consciousness and begin again by absorbing with your whole Be-ING the energy that is actively alive in that moment.

It is fear that blocks your consciousness, it is fear that puts you into sleep-state. Your Ego holds this fear within its perception; therefore, you are continuously battling to escape the fear in order to experience the moment. Even though you are not aware that you are doing this, you are! Your Ego tries to create reasons for your fears excuses for its negativity. This is because the Ego hides behind all the small fears in order to avoid its true fear, which is death. Your Egos do not want to face extinction from the Earth Plane, and so you occupy yourselves with multitudes of smaller fears. It is a diversion. The small fears camouflage the true fear (Death).

All of your fears are illusions, for your fears are created in mind. You occupy your mind with fears that have no foundation, no reality. Example: When you are fearful of meeting a new person, you are in mind fearing rejection that is not a reality. When you are fearful of riding a bicycle, you fear physical injury that has not yet manifested; therefore, it is not a reality. There are multitudes of fears that are illusions. The truest, realist, fear (because there is no exception to it) is death....so you live your lives hiding from this truth, and it creates your sleep-state. You render yourselves unconscious because your

Ego believes that if you hide from this truth, you will not be struck by it. What is needed is a conscious acceptance of this truth (which can only come about by releasing the perception of finality that the Ego holds) and to come into your God perception of eternal life, for this is Truth!

To embrace your whole Be-ING is to embrace your physical death, as well--to understand that you are not the Body to know that the dying of the body releases you from the limitations of the dense Ego plane....and to feel the freedom and the joy of continuing on to higher realms in order to experience your God-self as pure consciousness, will bring to you the freedom to embrace your experience of physical existence in a conscious state.

Questions asked in Group:

Q. How do we embrace death in order to release the fear of dying and enjoy living in the moment?

First, you must acknowledge that death is part of life, meaning that your death is always with you, is part of your Be-ING. Imagine your death as an energy that is waiting in the next room, and you know when you finish your work in the room where you are that you will go naturally to the next room to meet that part of you which is called `death`....and within that room you will experience yourself again in a new way, on a new level of consciousness.

When you come into life the Ego energy that surrounds you teaches you to ignore your death, for when you are growing no one sits with you and tells you that you are here for a short period of time and that you will die. No one speaks loudly to a young child or in front of a young child about an adult passing away; again, hiding this truth from you at every opportunity. Because the Ego sees death as finality, an ending, it fears it completely....and so you are taught to push it out of your mind and fight against the reality of it during your lifetime.

Now you have created a battle in your life that consumes your whole Be-ING because the effort to continuously push away your death robs you of your life. You are no longer free to enjoy the physical -- you are not free to trust your instincts -- you are not free to experience God and love openly. No matter how you try to experience these things, death is constantly a threat and you are always working to ignore its reality.

For example: You have deep difficulty in committing to a relationship. You believe through your Ego that this difficulty of commitment comes from some psychological place in your youth, your upbringing. Although these things may play a part, they are not the block. The block is your fear of dying; meaning, if you fear rejection, a commitment to a relationship will create more fear....so you will not commit. This is because rejection from a loved one means death to your energy. It is a form of dying an emotional death, and all forms of dying are being rejected by your Ego perception; therefore, you will not allow any death to surface in your consciousness and you will fight to keep buried whatever creates a death (be it an emotional death, a mental death, a spiritual death, or a physical one).

This is why you are unconscious in your physical existence. You must begin to understand here that from the moment you are born you are dying. As cells die off within your body and grow within your body, this dying and `birthing` is continuously happening in every moment of your physical life; therefore, many small deaths are taking place and many new births are also taking place. If an old idea is no longer believed, that idea has died. The new one that takes its place is a birth. The flow of this energy is what creates your life, your experience in the Earth Plane....and until the Be-ings of this <u>Plane</u> open their arms wide and embrace death, there will be unconsciousness -- no True life (consciousness) taking place in any Be-ING.

What is required is that Be-ings begin at the beginning with their young to explain death and how beautiful it is when the time is correct for the dying to take place, how precious life is, and the importance of preserving life as long as you can in order to learn all of your lessons, raise your consciousness, and become one with God. This may seem like very high, complicated, information to give to a child, but it is not! Children are more open to receive the truth because they have not yet lost connection to the `One` and they can assimilate the information and carry it with them throughout this physical life.

Fear creates limitation. It blocks the energy and it manifests decay - decay is not death.... decay is a distortion of the living, it is the mutilation of life! Death, however, is a journey into other realms of knowledge and wonder; and you must believe with all of your Be-ING that you are a manifestation of God, for this is the only truth that shall free you from your fear of death.

Q. I feel that I am conscious when I am working because I am aware of my boss's needs even as he speaks. I almost feel that I read his mind; so how can I be unconscious?

When you speak of your work, you are speaking of a structured environment, structured by the Ego perception of your boss, of yourself, and of the company that you work for. Within this structured environment, your Ego is confident because it is a repeated experience (as we have spoken about before) where the Ego becomes comfortable with whatever is repeated, and a structured work is where many things are repeated over and over again. Certain duties are repeated, certain expectations are fulfilled, and you are then able to do your work within your sleep-state as an airplane operates on automatic pilot. Your experiences in this position are clear and you instinctively know what is needed or what will be needed in the next moment, for the structure has taught you what to expect.

All jobs, for the most part, are structured and Be-ings can easily work in their sleep- state, for these jobs do not require your full attention after you have learned them well; however, when you are conscious and your full attention is present, the job is transformed and becomes more versatile and exciting and more possibilities are created. Even positions that call for spontaneity have a core structure that is followed, and the Ego adapts to this structure. Once adapted, it can go on automatic pilot. As in acting, in the profession of performance, an actor works out of a structure, a discipline, and if he is an average performer it is because he is not conscious within every moment, he is relying on the structure to carry him--and it does! When an actor is brilliant it is only because he goes beyond the structure and he is conscious in every moment, allowing new life, new energy, and expansion to take place, creating a more vivid and moving character.

Your Ego is good at fooling you into believing that you are conscious when you are not. You, yourself, will recognize isolated moments of consciousness at your work wherever you discover something right in the moment that changes the direction of a project or a letter. These isolated moments of consciousness are called `revelations,` strokes of genius, and the Ego pays great homage to those who have them....when, in truth, consciousness is available to everyone, but through the Ego perception it is a rare gift of insight.

Q. At times when I am conscious and able to pick up on someone's energy, I find that I see truths about that energy that are not manifested in the person's manner of speaking and acting. This causes me unhappiness because I do not feel free to confront that person without proof of my insights. It is a difficult choice, do I not trust and, therefore, not act upon my insights or do I trust them and go forward in approaching that person?

The difficulty in the choice is trusting. You have difficulty trusting yourself, so, therefore, there is always a doubt in your mind....and when you have insights (no matter how powerful they are) that alter your reality, you are hesitant in believing them to be true. Understand that your insights are not always pure because you have an Ego perception; however, when you are conscious they are pure....but because you are not always clear about this, you may believe that you are conscious when you are not....therefore, you must always check out your instincts, your intuition.

Acknowledge to yourself that you have this insight, that, you are picking up information that is not being spoken but which you are sensing within the energy. Hold this information.

Do not jump forward with it until you can prove its reality. How do you do this? By knowing what the insight is....you are armed with knowledge that will create a deeper awareness of the situation that you are in with this other Be-ING.... and as time passes, your interactions with this Be-ING will begin to reveal the truthfulness of your insight, if it is purely a True insight. This is meaning, something shall manifest, shall surface, to confirm this belief and at that point you are free to go forward with the information, not only information of the moment but also information that you have stored through your instinctual understanding of this Be-ING.

There are only few moments in a Be-ings life that are clearly conscious, when there is an opening within the mind that allows you to see your connection to God. In those moments, there is no doubt that you are conscious. There are also moments that your insights work to alert you to danger and you are compelled to follow them.

When you are dealing with Be-ings of the Earth Plane, you are always dealing with Ego perception....so you must be cautious for you can create separation and pain in the Emotional Body if you are not coming from a conscious state. You are not yet at a level of consciousness where you can know that which exists in truth in <u>every</u> moment.

Q. Does being conscious mean that you are able to read the energy around people and things?

When you are conscious, this is meaning that you are present in the moment -- when you are present, you possess all of the wisdom, the knowledge, of the moment. This is meaning that consciousness brings you into a Godly state....and within this state nothing escapes you - you are able to know the energies through your senses, meaning that you know without speaking, without being told you know through <u>feeling</u> the energy if something is safe or unsafe, if it is a pleasant situation or unpleasant.

There have been Be-ings, while within consciousness, who have been able to sense the energy of a negative spirit in a room, for example, and they do not see the spirit nor do they hear it, yet they feel it throughout their whole Be-ING and describe it as if the energy in the room becomes heavy, that energy has a weight and they feel that weight. Through their eyes they see the colors in the room darken, almost as if sunglasses were placed on their eyes....and they are in complete knowing that there is a negative spirit present....they know what is needed and they immediately call in the White Light. They call for their God-self to enter the space. They do not have to do this with words, they call it with their energy through the mind.... and the Light immediately comes into the room, the energy is sensed as becoming lighter, and the visual becomes brighter. This is one example of what is known as being in a highly conscious state.

In the Physical World (in the Ego) you begin to see the Ego much clearer for you hear beneath what is said. In other words, perhaps someone is saying to you, `I like you very much,` and perhaps they do <u>not</u> like you. When you are conscious, you hear within those words that they do not mean what they say. You see through this because the Body cannot lie and sound and vibration are One with God -- you can hear within the sound and the vibration of what is being said: the True meaning.

You cannot do this unless you are conscious. Nothing escapes you when you are in conscious state. A gesture of the Body speaks in its own language, operates by itself, because, again, the movement is energy and your body instinctively moves and takes positions that are in alignment with the energy that is present….so if a Be-ING is trying to hide, perhaps, that he is shy and fearful of your energy, his body movements will tell on him and you will know this if you are conscious enough to see the movements and to interpret their meaning.

Interpretation is immediately present with the movement or the restriction of the Physical Body. Being able to connect to all your Heavenly bodies will clearly tell you what is taking place in every moment and what is needed to serve that moment. For example, when you are aware that someone is shy and fearful of you, you are able to position your energy in such a way that they no longer feel threatened or fearful….so you serve the energy, serve the moment, by making an adjustment in your own energy.

With this knowledge, you do not fall to the Ego's fears, doubts, and game-playing, because you are able to extract the joy and the power within that moment. In each moment that you are conscious you absorb the power and the joy, you become more likened to your True Self, you become more God and less Ego….joy is God--fear is Ego-- and consciousness is what will bring you into this realization!

Q. If I were conscious in every moment, how would my life be different?

Your life would be different in many ways. First, you would no longer possess fear, and without fear you would possess joy. You would no longer have expectations because you would trust every moment, for everything would be clear to you in every moment….and trust would come naturally to your energy. There would be no anxiety over your work or your relationships, for your consciousness would always alert you to any negative energy that might be present within that work or relationship….in being alert, you would easily be able to diffuse the negativity and replace it with positive love energy.

Your life would be as it is meant to be, a life of learning of realizations that bring you closer to your God-self….and you would become a true reflection of the Creator. Everything you touch, everything you experience within all of your Bodies, would be raised to its `Highest` form and your world would be manifested as a `Heaven on Earth` for your Be-ING. Even though other Be-ings still would be within their Ego perception, you would rise above the negativity by creating for yourself a conscious existence.

Anna's Thoughts: Consciousness (Awareness)

Our fear of physical death through Ego creates to the greatest extent our unconsciousness and our inability to stay in the moment, for death is our ultimate fear. We cannot control this ultimate fear and it causes us to fall deeper into our illusions, where we try to escape it through the creation of fears that we feel we can manage and control. This is how we give ourselves a false sense of security that we are in control of our mortality. How do we do this?

Example: I draw here a parallel between fear of flying in an airplane, vs. the ultimate fear of death (flight from the physical into the unknown). Fear of flying is one of our created fears with which we occupy ourselves. Conquering them is sometimes difficult; however, it is not impossible. By placing ourselves in the experience of flying and learning everything there is to know about it, we can overcome our fear of it. It is the <u>experience</u> that truly frees us. We cannot, however, place ourselves in the experience of mortal death and trust that we will conquer it; that is the reason it is the ultimate fear.

In attempting to conquer the ultimate fear, man may be, for example, compelled to explore outer space; thereby reaching beyond the physical into the unknown in order to ground it into his physical reality. <u>The unknown becomes known.</u> Man strives to know his own death in order to overcome the fear of it. Man's constant striving for this knowledge traps him deeper within his fear of death and blocks his awareness in life.

We are delinquent in a never-ending pursuit of the unknown; and so long as we chase the illusive butterfly, we will continue to miss the reality of our physical existence. Earth is our domain. God gives us the Earth and the body that we occupy for a short expansion of time. We ignore the gift of life by not living it. We do not live life because we are trapped in the fear of losing it. When we learn to trust that death is an extension of life, we will be able to relinquish our attempts to control the physical life and then surrender to the love that is continuously creating it.

SEVENTH INGREDIENT: COMMITMENT (RESPONSIBILITY)

*Be-ings of the Earth Plane have difficulty with commitment and responsibility. This difficulty comes because there is so much permanence in the word `commitment` for the Egos `energy,` and this permanence creates fear. This is because the

Ego is constantly working to out-maneuver its death, meaning, as we spoke before, that your Ego energy fears its own death and continuously works to suppress this fear. Therefore, if the Ego needs to stay in a commitment, this means its energy is focused and it is fearful of death catching up to it. This is complicated to understand on the surface but, in truth, it is simple to understand, for the Ego, fearing its own death, also fears commitment. Commitment captures the energy and the Ego feels trapped within the commitment because it believes if it is not continuously dodging the ultimate fear, it will be discovered by the Angel of Death and eliminated.

This is a very deep-core reason for the fear of commitment that many Be-ings possess. It does not mean that some Be-ings have not overcome this fear and have joyfully committed themselves to be responsible Be-ings through their relationships within their families and their work and in service to their communities. These are Be-ings whose fear of death does not run as deeply as those who cannot commit; nonetheless, they still possess this fear of commitment to a degree.

When you are committed, for example, to a job and a time arises where within the job there are problems and there is possibility that you may lose your position, at these points the fear rises and the Be-ING may immediately abandon the commitment in order to preserve' himself.` You might say he is not abandoning his commitment but that his commitment is abandoning him; but, in truth, his fear is abandoning him, for he believes if he loses his position he no longer will have an identity, he will not be able to hold up his head in his community, he will lose respect from his family....and it becomes a life-threatening situation for his Ego....so he abandons that commitment in order to find a new position so that he does not lose his image. This is the Ego not the God- consciousness which is directing his energy, for if it were the God-consciousness he would not be motivated by his fear (death), he would be motivated by love (life), and would trust in the outcome.

One might re-act the same in `personal` relationships. Those who are in deeper fear cannot commit to a relationship (one that is of intimacy) with another Be-ING. Those with lesser fear commit to relationships, but the commitment is fragile and anything that enters into the relationship (that creates fear of loss or rejection, and so forth) could become motivation to release the commitment. This is one reason why so many Be-ings on the Earth Plane do not survive their marriages…. because they are threatened through their Ego perception and, therefore, `run for their lives,` as you might say. Also many who commit out of the Ego's fear, remain in loveless situations because they fear being alone and unprotected. Here exists the belief: that in their commitment they are successfully hiding from death and cannot be found. This fear is powerful for it robs you of your joy and peace, of True life itself, creating your own imprisonment.

Only a Be-ING who is centered in his energy and aligned to his God-self can create a commitment that is lasting, for it is based in love and trust, therefore, there is no fear of death motivating this energy.

As we spoke before of all the small deaths that your energy experiences, we now address the discrimination in this, for you may fear certain deaths more than others. In other words, in

your energy, you may fear emotional death much more than a
mental death, meaning mental energies, thought patterns, loss
of belief systems, and so forth.

The only one true fear of death is of the Physical Body, yet
there are no Be-ings who only fear physical death. Why?
Because the physical dying of the body is seen and experienced
in all the smaller deaths within your energy. Why this is, is
because you are energy and you are of the `One` energy. You
cannot separate this fear from any part of your energy without
eliminating it completely from your perception.

So you must see that in order to eliminate this fear from your
Ego perception, you must come out of your Ego perception
of death. The Ego and this fear are connected `at the hip,`
as you might say, and you cannot remain in this perception
and become an enlightened Be-ING. Here is where you
can begin to use the power of the ingredients, `commitment
and responsibility`....for as you open your heart to receive
the love energy, you will take responsibility to keep this love
alive in every moment....and in order to do this, you must
make a commitment to yourself, commitment to your healing,
commitment to your enlightenment, commitment to your
own power....then you shall be creating in every moment the
energy that you are, in Truth.

Making a commitment to oneself through the love energy is
focusing in your God-consciousness where you then cannot
be abandoned by your Ego. Only when you focus in your Ego-
consciousness and you make a commitment to continue in the
Ego's belief system, can you be hurt or destroyed by your Ego.
Being able to see yourself as you are, in truth, God energy,

you are then able to understand clearly all that is being taught about the energies, which you experience in and through the Physical Plane.

Begin now to work on consciously making the commitment to heal yourself, to love yourself, and to raise yourself in this life in order to experience the creation in God-consciousness.

Questions asked on Commitment:

Q. If I am fearful of commitment to another and I believe this fear comes from my upbringing because my parents separated when I was growing up, how do I overcome the fear in order to make a commitment?

In order to do this, you are needing to change your perception, for you are now perceiving yourself through your parents.... you are seeing yourself as they are rather than as you are, in Truth. Many Be-ings in the Earth Plane do this because the Ego becomes attached to the past and to the familiar actions of those closest to its energy; therefore, you do not see your individuality even though you believe that you are an individual, for, in truth, you believe that whatever took place with your parents will certainly take place with you.

That belief creates the feeling of `all-knowing,` so you know if you make the commitment you will suffer pain and separation....even though your God-consciousness recognizes the harmony and the beauty in this union, your Ego-consciousness only sees the pain and immediately blocks your ability to commit.

It is difficult for the Ego to let go of all the impressions that created fear and threatened its existence....but with the new wisdom that you possess as energy (as the Creator of your own life) you can go forward and make your commitment with faith and trust, that even though it may end up in physical separation, it will serve you, teach you, and raise your awareness through the experience (that you have created) of committing your energy to a union.

What is being said is there are no set results in any commitment. A commitment can prove to be `long-lasting` and peaceful, and a commitment can prove to be painful and filled with karmic lessons, and the reason for this is you are `energy` moving through physical matter. A `long-lasting` commitment is a commitment where the energy may continue to grow in unison, or in discord, therefore, creating all of the virtues of your God-self, or the limitations of your Ego-self. A commitment that is `short-lived,` is energy that dies quickly within this combination. There are multitudes of reasons why Be-ings are brought together for only short periods of time. Know that within those periods, the Be- ING has moved to a new understanding of `himself` therefore, there is nothing more at that point to learn or to keep the energies alive in the union. The learning experience within any union may be hidden from your consciousness, yet it is absorbed by the Soul Energy of your Be-ING. The outcome is not the point....it is not where the value of the commitment lies. The value is within the experience, moment by moment....it is the journey that you take within that commitment from which you grow, from which you gain wisdom, which nurtures and raises the consciousness of your Whole Be-ING.

An ending to a commitment is only the end of a journey. Once a journey ends, another begins, so do not focus on the outcome. Focus on the journey, focus in the moment…. for within the moment lies the True commitment!

Q. Are you saying that a commitment does not necessarily mean `forever,` that it is not for life?

It is because your Ego is all-knowing and it believes in outcomes and expectations that you see a commitment as something that has a fulfillment of eternity attached to it. The only commitment that is eternal is your commitment to your God-self.

When you speak of `for life` in the Earth Plane, you must understand that all energy has its own life. When you light a candle, that energy has its own life in that it will burn out in a certain number of hours. The energy between you and another Be-ING has its own life, as well. If it is a business partner, you will work until business is complete, the life is then over. If it is a commitment to a mother, father, or sibling, this energy also has its own life; the life expectancy with these commitments, however, is usually longer because your energy and the energies of these Be-ings have chosen one another before you came into Body, to work on balancing deep emotional Karma in this life. Even so, many times a sibling relationship, for example, is `short-lived` when a balance cannot be achieved and the relationship becomes a block to further personal growth and the relationship then must be released. If it is a marriage, you will work as long as it takes within that union to come to your God perception your God-consciousness. If a point is reached within the marriage where you can no longer sustain your True-self the marriage may end.

What is meant here is that a personal, intimate relationship is either growing into a higher consciousness and, therefore, continues on or it is growing within Ego-consciousness and, therefore, the life span of the relationship is shortened....for every Be-ING is manifested in order to come into the light of Truth which is approached, reached, in many different ways, meaning many paths to God are taken.

When you look at one element within your path, you are narrowing your vision to believe that your wholeness rests on that one element alone. Your intimate relationship with another is only one more element in your whole Be-ING, in your whole experience in this life. Therefore, if you see this through your God-consciousness you will recognize that everything in the Physical Plane has an ending....a beginning, middle, and an ending. The only thing that is eternal is the `One` energy `God!` In order for you to continue in the Light, you must continuously move through the lessons that are created out of your Ego-consciousness, for only through this movement can you remain connected to the light of your True self (God-self).

Your eternal self is your God-self....and in order to come into this truth, you must let go of your Ego's fears and attachments by accepting what takes place in your energy, moving through the negativity that you see....you will then create a deeper love for self. Do not punish yourself; rather, nurture your Be-ING with love for your own energy.... which allows you to see more clearly that you must let go in order for you to go on.

Q. How can I live within the Light of love for (Self) while competing in the Ego world?

You do this by changing your perception. This is meaning, you do not perceive yourself in competition, for you are not in Truth when you are in competition with another part of your energy. Knowing that you are energy, that all is of the `One` energy, you seek cooperation with your energy....you do not conflict with your own energy. This perception allows you to see that while you are within the light of love for self, you are able to raise the energy of the physical world through your positive actions within it and your loving approach to the Ego perception of self and others.

For example: If you are in line for a promotion at your job and there are five others in the same position, you do not perceive the others as inferior or superior to yourself. You focus your energy on being the best that you can possibly be at your work, and you do not hide your Light....you let your Light be known to everyone at your job....you let it be known through your actions, your performance, not through tearing down others or lying or creating conflict, for that is competing and this creates separation.

By living within the Light you receive what you need, and if you need to gain the position, you shall. If you are not to receive the position, you shall continue without resentment or anger, for you will know that your energy is growing....and moving towards a position that is not yet in its manifestation. This takes a great deal of trusting that your Ego is not accustomed to; yet only through trusting that your energy is being guided by your God-self, will you be accepting that which manifests.

Understand this clearly: In order to live within the Light and rise above the Ego-consciousness, you must trust and you must love yourself. You must live in the perception of Truth, that your energy is of the `One energy` and that you are experiencing through the physical form the power of the Creative Force. You are always creating and you must take responsibility for your creations in order to direct your creativity into its highest form.

Q. I feel that in taking responsibility for myself causes me sometimes to neglect others. Am I being selfish?

When you are taking responsibility for your own Be-ING you do not neglect any part of the Whole within the moment; so, therefore, when you are neglecting that which is in the moment it is because you are not taking responsibility, in truth....you are obsessed with fear and that fear creates an attachment to the self (meaning the Physical Ego-self) wherein you are worried about your energy. Only worry and fear can block out what is taking place in every moment.

When you are within true responsibility, you are not fearful and you are then free to address whatever is present. If another Be-ING is in need of attention, whether it be positive, or negative, you are present in that moment.... and you are free to serve that Be-ING. If you are needing to give from an emotional plane, you are able because you are taking care of yourself, in truth, when you are open and consciously available in every moment.

Be-ings of the Earth Plane do not understand clearly what it means to take care of their own energy. They believe it means to protect themselves from harm, from others....and this perception is of fear - fear creates separation. When you are

truly taking care of yourself, you are including the Whole....
you are available....and this does not mean that you cannot
say, `I need private time to myself.` This is something that
your energy may need to do in the moment, and so long as
you clearly state your needs within the moment you are taking
responsibility for your actions. It is when you are not clear
that you create confusion and negative emotions. So giving to
yourself what you need must come from a conscious state not
a fearful one. In that way, you are not being selfish rather, you
are serving the Self (Higher-self).

*Q. If I see a loved one either acting or dressing in a way that I
feel might cause him embarrassment, I would not only feel it my
responsibility to shield him from that embarrassment by telling
him of my feelings, but also would feel guilty in not doing so.*

When we speak of responsibility, we are speaking of taking
responsibility for the Self. As we have said, you cannot take
responsibility for another Be-ING, only for your own energy;
therefore, when you see something that you believe will cause
embarrassment to someone else, you must see that this is a
belief that you hold through your own experiences....through
your own upbringing.

When you are a child your parents take responsibility for
you because you are not able to take care of yourself. This is
the time that you learn how to take care of yourself through
what you are taught. If you are taught well you know how to
protect yourself from embarrassment by doing what is correct
within the moment. If you do not know this, it is because you
have not absorbed the lesson that teaches you how to care for
yourself in the correct way. Therefore, when you are an adult

and you dress in a bizarre way it is because you are needing the attention; whether it be positive or negative attention is of no consequence to a Be-ING who is needing the attention. The lesson is to discover that there is a need here and learn how to serve the need from within, rather than from without.

See clearly that when you interfere with someone's choices, you are interfering with their lesson....you are interfering with their growth....for they are creating the experience that will teach them what perhaps the parent did not and this must be their responsibility not yours. This is how you show love for them, in truth, by giving the space that is needed for their enlightenment. You have a saying, `love with your arms opened wide.` That means, do not impose your desires, your tastes, or your understanding upon another Be-ING. Only give what is asked for. This means when someone asks for your opinion you are then free to give it, for the asking is part of one's learning. If one does not ask, one is not prepared to receive; so one must not attempt to speed up the pace of the energy in another person's lesson. This is love, in Truth, unconditional!

Anna's Thoughts: Commitment (Responsibility)

We, all people of the Earth, consist of a masculine and a feminine side to our energy. These two sides are out of balance in most individuals and this imbalance causes conflict between men and women. This is due to the fact that the feminine side of our nature is drawn to union, whereas the masculine side is drawn to separation. Herein lays our conflict. When the masculine side of our energy dominates our Be-ING we fear commitment and continuously work to create our individuality, this separates us one from another; the feminine side of our energy, however, seeks to unite with our outer reflection, ultimately desiring to create balance and peace.

The feminine side of our nature is where we are connected through the Emotional Body and the masculine side through the Ego Body. In order for us to be in perfect harmony with both our inner self and our outer world, we must first balance the Yin and Yang within.

I am beginning to see how the fear coming through the Ego blocks each and every one of us from creating true union within ourselves and with others; if we have no `True union` with ourselves or (with God), we cannot create a true union with another person. When we look at ourselves as the men and women of today's world, we find that through our lack of consciousness we are irresponsible in almost every area of our lives; for example, sometimes in the care of our physical bodies. As we are well aware, a great number of people in our society have some type of eating disorder. We can now see that it is due to the conflict caused by the imbalance of the masculine and feminine energy within, which creates anxiety. We are continuously worrying about our appearance because we believe that we are not attractive enough to create union with another, or we hide in our appearance by creating one that is undesirable and, therefore, protects us from the entrapment that we perceive union to be; hence, eating disorders.

Whenever we become fearful of sharing intimacy and we feel the urge to take flight, we are experiencing the feminine and masculine energy in conflict because the fear comes from the Emotional Body and the flight is the action that manifests through the Ego Body. The desire for intimacy comes from the feminine side; the masculine side creates the fear in the emotion that ultimately manifests the flight. This is taking place in each individual, so when you see how it manifests between men and women as separate individuals, you will see that the majority of the male energy (the man) is lacking emotional awareness and the female (the woman) is deeply connected, sometimes to a fault, to her emotional experiences; therefore, when you put men and women together they are incapable of being totally honest with one another. It is impossible to trust from the female perspective that the male will not minimize her intelligence due to her emotional connection; and it is very difficult for the male to trust that the female will not block him from experiencing his freedom to be mobile in the physical world. This deep lack of trust is a manifestation of the inner lack of trust that comes through our inner conflict. So when we speak of commitment and responsibility we are speaking first of 'Self'-commitment.

Truly, ASTRA is saying that we must be committed to ourselves in order to create union between the masculine and the feminine sides within our own Be-ING, experiencing inner union that enables us to take responsibility for manifesting a union with another. Once we create this inner union, we are <u>total</u> Be-ings because we give to ourselves everything we need: To be self-contained, emotionally, physically, mentally and spiritually, we would no longer live in the conflict as we do now. Only then could we unite with one another and trust that intimacy does not block movement and freedom in our lives, but rather creates it.

EIGHTH INGREDIENT: DISCRIMINATION

*What does the word `discrimination` mean? Through the Ego perception, the word means to either eliminate or separate `yourself` from a person, place or thing. The Ego uses discrimination as a form of prejudice. That is not, however, the true meaning of discrimination. The true function of discrimination is using free choice to choose something of a higher nature, whether it be a material, spiritual or emotional choice....this is the true meaning of discrimination!

In order to exercise your free choice in all things, you must learn to discriminate by being conscious of what exists within the positive and negative energies, for both positive and negative exist in every moment....and only when you are a conscious Be-ING are you free to discriminate between the positive and negative.

As an example, when you are a youth and you are confronted by your peers to participate in negative behavior by taking drugs, performing criminal acts against others, and so forth. If you are a conscious Be-ING you are able to discriminate without fear, allowing you to reject the negativity not only for yourself but also for the Whole, recognizing that your involvement in these actions draws down the energy of the One....you are then free to discriminate and choose to separate your energy from the negativity by joining your energy to a higher purpose. This is what true discrimination is!

The Ego has difficulty in using discrimination for the good of the Whole because it is filled with fear. Fear of judgment gives the Ego permission to join in the negativity; and because of this, true discrimination is not present.

So recognize that it is the Ego's fear that blocks true discrimination, for the Ego chooses through fear rather than love. It is only your God-self that is able to discriminate, for your God-self holds love for all of Creation....and this is how discrimination against that which is harmful to the Creation is followed. Understanding that your energy is of the One, you are freeing your Be-ING from fear of judgment....and you are now able to use the ingredient `discrimination` to create a world of love and peace for yourself and others.

Your Ego might believe that discrimination is creating separation in that saying `this is good for me` and `this is bad for me` separates the energy. To answer this, I will say, visualize a huge pot filled with energy of positive nature and negative nature, of darkness and light, of fear and love, of sorrow and joy, of pain and delight. Now take a huge wooden spoon and stir all of these energies together and know that the Creator God has allowed all of this to manifest, for it has all come from Mind and, therefore, has been created as an extension of the One (God).

Now visualize that you, as the Creator, have manifested your physical form and are then added to the ingredients of energy. You hold the Creative Power through your connection to the One Mind of God, and when you use your power to create balance within the energy you are working in God-Consciousness; therefore, you are not separating evil from good, sorrow from joy, you are using your discrimination to transform evil into good and sorrow into joy, uniting the energy through your discrimination rather than separating it. As a good chef adds complimentary ingredients to his soup in order to create a nurturing and palatable taste of sheer delight, you are the chef in creating balance, nurturing palatable energy in every conceivable expression of the One.

Questions asked about Discrimination in class:

Q. Would you call it `True` discrimination when you stop seeing a friend who does something negative towards you?

When there is a separation of energy as in the ending of a relationship with a friend, this takes place on many levels of your Be-ING. First, it takes place within the Emotional Body and there are many feelings that may create a separation that are not within the Light, for many Be-ings separate out of the Ego's perception wherein emotions are directed through the Ego's fear....and you believe something negative was done against your person when it might not be so in truth. This is why you must remain conscious in every moment in order to know if you are within Truth.

In order to truly discriminate through the Emotional Body you must be conscious of what exists in the energies of this friendship and you must be free from fear in order to confront (with love) the friend and clear away any misunderstanding in order to discriminate within the Light. If you are to find that this Be-ING truly turned against your energy, then you will see that this relationship has died, for it cannot continue any longer when one party has lost love for the other. Without love there is no creativity, without creativity there is no life; therefore, in order for your energy to continue in life, it will have to move away from the relationship.

Q. I feel that many people have a distorted interpretation of the meaning of discrimination, those who believe they must preserve their religion, race, tradition, etc., by living a `clannish` way of life to the extent that they mistrust those of different beliefs and appearance.

The reason this takes place is because, as we have spoken before, the Ego is attached to the past, to what is familiar. It feels safe within familiarity and threatened when it is confronted with something different, unfamiliar. Be-ings of the Earth Plane within their Ego perception are trapped within past behavior. In your beginning you lived in tribes, tribes of religion, color and of the region. You were threatened by other tribes and you needed to protect yourselves from invasion. This created the belief that in coming together with your ancestors you were able to trust because you lived with people of like-mind.

As the world evolved, many changes took place. The world became smaller and you could easily move to another region where people of different cultures lived. People began to move from one place to another and, because of the Ego's perception within fear, began to create small tribes within the new territory. Small ethnic groups sprung up in the same area within unfamiliar ethnic groups. There was less physical space between the tribes, and a breeding of negativity and hatred developed because of the close proximity of Be-ings who were holding different ethnic and spiritual beliefs.

All this takes place because your Ego will not let go of the familiar past. Your Ego is holding back your growth as Spiritual Be-ings by creating conflict within its own space. Example: A race of people of different color and tradition moves into an area. They build their camp. They do not attempt to learn about their new territory and the people within it in order to meld with them and grow in a new direction. Instead, they fight to preserve a small space and, therefore, they contaminate their own space for they invite hatred and mistrust to themselves from the natives of that land.

It is important for people to come into their God-consciousness in order to embrace the differences between them, to see the beauty in those differences, to learn more about love and trust through sharing of beliefs and traditions. This does not mean that a Be-ING must give up his traditions in order to belong in this new area. It means he must share himself in order for the others to feel safe in his presence. Only that which is kept in secret creates mistrust and fear in the Ego. When you are open and you share who you are with others, you become one who can be understood and, therefore, trusted.

The reason there is so much hatred is because peoples of the Earth are living in the past and they believe themselves to be better than others, to be correct in their beliefs, therefore, seeing others as incorrect. This sets up the conflict immediately. There is no correct or incorrect tradition or religious belief, nor specific way that one should look (color, size, shape, accent and so forth.) all are an expression of the Creator God.

As we have said before, God manifests in multitudes of ways and every Be-ING is God-manifested in the Earth Plane. Every Be-ING is part of the `One energy,` for every Be-ING is the `One` energy, `God.` To place one above the other is to give away the power, the light, of your True self. To open your heart and embrace your whole Be-ING is to open yourself to learn about everyone and everything in the Creation.

Yes, there is negativity the negative and positive exist together. You are not being told that you are to be blinded to this darkness. What is being said here is that you must accept the darkness, for only through accepting it can your creative force come through your Be-ING and create Light where there is darkness. This is meaning to change your world. Creating balance between people moves the energy forward to create balance within the Planet, itself, within nature….and this balance will raise the creativity of every living Be-ING on this planet.

In order to do this, there can only be one clan and that clan is the spiritual clan, the like mindedness of every Be-ING in spirit. Knowing that you are all energy, you are all a manifestation of God and you are all working together in love, to create beyond what you experience at this time….for in this present time your minds are blocked by hatred, fear, anger and all of the negative forces so that your creativity is limited. True discrimination is when at any time that you see yourself blocking out a Be-ING because of his race, religious beliefs, physical appearance, and so forth, you stop and you discriminate in Truth, by accepting that difference….seeing that which is positive within it, opening yourself to understand the true value that is before you. It will take great courage to face your own beliefs, prejudices, and fears; yet every Be-ING is manifested at this time to come into the Light through experiencing his own Creations of darkness.

Q. I believe that wars are caused by false discrimination. For example, in Ireland people hate one another due to different religious beliefs. I feel that false discrimination is affecting all forms of spirituality. Is this true?

It is true that the Ego creates discrimination in all things. The religious beliefs of a Be- ING are the most sensitive areas for attack through Ego perception, for a Be-ING is connected through spirit to his creativity….and when his spirituality is attacked his creativity is attacked and it creates great conflict in that a Be-ING is made to feel compelled to fight for his honor. This is, of course, again, the Ego that motivates this feeling.

In Ireland the Be-ings are within conflict through their religious beliefs only because religion is involved in all aspects of life. In other words, their religious organizations do not work only within spirit; they are also working within politics and that is why there is a sensitivity that manifests violence, meaning it is safer to attack through the Ego on a political plane alone. Once your spirituality and creativity is attacked along with your political structure and views, it is like manifesting an atom bomb, and bloodshed is surely to take place.

Your spirituality is the `Mani-fester` of that which is created for the highest good within the Physical World. When your spirituality becomes involved with the politics of the Ego it loses its true power, for the Ego manipulates the spirit in this union. Remember that within the physical world the Ego holds the power. It is difficult to see clearly what is being said because you are told that God is the power and how you perceive is what manifests your world, and this is truth; yet within the physical dense energy of the Earth Plane there is separation from spirit and the Ego rules. Every institution, every political structure, has been created out of the Ego perception; therefore, if religious organizations align themselves to these structures they are giving their power over to the Ego.

In order to change the world as it is today one must see this clearly: Remain in your spiritual perception and do not become absorbed in the present world of the Ego….and you will be free to restructure the world. All forms of negativity in your justice system, for example, can only be changed not by interference of your spiritual beliefs, not by aligning your spiritual beliefs with the present structure but by living the spiritual Truth in your own world, in your own life. If every Be-ING keeps sacred his spiritual energy he will rise above the manifestations that exist within the Ego-consciousness.... then the power of the Truth will expand from one Be-ING to another until all Be-ings of like mind in spirit will be `One.` At that point changes will take place within the judicial system as within other systems that have been created through your Ego perception.

Oil and water do not mix! Therefore, Ego and your God-self must become one, for the spiritual perception and the Ego perception do not mix - they are of two separate minds. This separateness is what creates the pain and chaos within your Earth Plane. See this clearly: The Ego is pulling the Spirit into its creations in order to gain complete power. It is trying to block your Spiritual Body to survive and preserve the physical illusion....so it is of the utmost concern that man remain true to his Spirit, and allow the power of God to manifest within the Ego, aligning the Ego to Spirit rather than having Spirit blocked by the Ego, for this is what is taking place within your Earth Plane. Your Ego is devouring your Spiritual Body by blocking it, and you must pull out of the Ego's grip in order to save the creation of Earth.

Q. Can you give us a guideline on how to recognize within ourselves when we are in true discrimination and when we are not; and when we are not, how to release that desire to discriminate in a negative way?

To recognize true discrimination within your own Be-ING is simple. Know that when you are choosing you are within discrimination....when there is a choice to be made between things, behavior, ideas, goals, and so forth, for the self. Examples: (1) do you eat eggs or do you eat ice cream for your morning meal? You are discriminating between the eggs and the ice cream. This is a true discrimination because it either serves or does not serve you, in that your choice benefits or does not benefit your Physical Body. (2) Do you visit your mother who is ill or do you go to a ball game with a friend? You are discriminating between choices. This is a true discrimination because it either serves or does not serve the Emotional Body. Both examples are true discrimination because they are for the self.

When you discriminate for someone else, however, you are within darkness. This is not true discrimination. Example: If you tell someone, `don't wear the blue dress wear the green one,` you are choosing for someone else and this is not in Truth. You must always allow others to choose for themselves. In the same way, when you discriminate against a race of people, you are not serving the self, for you are cutting off your own energy. Why? Because all is `One` energy, and when you cut off a race of people, it is likened to cutting off your own arm. In cutting off a limb, it is clear that you are separating from your own energy. When you cut off a race of people, the Ego believes this discrimination to be serving, for it believes that it is separate from other Be-ings....this belief in separation is what creates negative discrimination. When you are understanding this, you are within the Light, you see the simplicity, for it is simple. When you discriminate for your own Be-ING by serving the self within the moment, you are in true discrimination.

I shall clarify this more. If you are walking down a street in an area that is unfamiliar and you sense danger from certain people there, you discriminate in that moment and you remove yourself from the area, this is true discrimination, for you are being guided by your instincts to preserve the self. If you are at a party, however, and you see someone who is of the same color as those you encountered in the area of danger and you discriminate against this person for that one reason-- this is <u>not</u> true discrimination, for you are linking this person to the predictive negative energy, by the color of his skin rather than the nature of his Be-ING. This discrimination is of the negative Ego perception and it only serves to separate you from your True Self.

You know that you are within negative discrimination when you are experiencing prejudice within that discrimination. When you believe that something is superior to something else, that something is good and something is bad this is negative discrimination, for in truth all energy is of the One.... therefore, it is all positive in its Truest form. When it is broken down into physical manifestation it becomes an illusion that one thing is different from another. It only seems that way through the Ego's perception; in other words, it is the Ego's discriminating in its act of prejudice against that which it does not understand -- does not accept -- and fears to experience.

Within True discrimination there is no prejudice. The choice is made to serve the moment, that which suits the moment best is chosen and there is no negative energy directed at what is <u>not </u>chosen. EXAMPLE: If you choose not to associate with a person because he is interfering with your work in the moment, you are discriminating without prejudice in that your choice is to serve your work and there is no negative prejudice against the person. Everything must be created to serve the moment. When you are within service of the moment you are within the Light, you are not rejecting any part of the Creation. You are consciously serving that which exists within the moment in which you are.

Man must learn to unite his energy so he may be powerful within the Light of Truth, of Spirit. The separation of energy that the Ego creates is what keeps man in darkness and perpetuates decay.

ANNA'S THOUGHTS: DISCRIMINATION

Discrimination is a powerful ingredient. When seen through the highest consciousness (God) it is expressed in its truest form and enlightens us to choose that which elevates the self and unites the Whole. When seen through the lower self (Ego), however, discrimination creates separation and prejudice manifests. As ASTRA says, we have come to believe, through Ego, the false meaning of discrimination which is to freely exercise our prejudice and create separation for selfish gain. With full understanding of the true meaning of discrimination, however, we are able to make the powerful connection of that which exists in the moment to that of free choice (the true companion of discrimination), and we would no longer choose arbitrarily that which our Ego desires or that which we may be talked into by another; rather, we would choose through True discrimination that which is of the highest good and which would serve the Whole. When the Whole of Creation is our main focus, discrimination serves us to choose well.

I know that we are powerful, and that through True discrimination we are able to create understanding and compassion--this is exciting! We need to make the connection to the power of all `ingredients` within us, and to follow the thread of love that unites them. Only then can we see that acceptance brings compassion, truth creates trust, and our love creates intimacy with the Whole (God). We will then recognize our perfection and see that our truest need is to stay in remembrance of love for self.

Ninth Ingredient: Courage

*The ninth ingredient is courage....for it is the power of your ability to unite with your courage that manifests all of the ingredients that you possess. It takes courage to love--it takes courage to choose that which is of the highest nature--it takes courage to be responsible, to make commitments and to discriminate in Truth. <u>Courage</u> is `energy` of great force. It is what moves you through the density of the Earth Plane. It moves you through the fear that the `Ego` creates--for the greatest courage of all is to face your fears and transform the illusion into the reality of the true nature of all things.

When you open yourself in the heart Chakra to receive all of the vibrations put forth by others, you are acting within the light of courage....for in choosing to open your heart in spite of the Ego's desire to keep it closed and protected from the negativity that the Ego has created.... you are going forward in trust that Love will triumph over hatred. The deepest courage of all, however, is the courage to go within your own Be-ING and to face your own demons of darkness....to see your Ego perception and to take responsibility for the creation of your life within the Earth Plane....to take responsibility for your emotions and the healing of the child within your Be-ING….and to forgive yourself for all that has passed through your Ego perception. This all takes courage.

Where does this courage come from? It comes from the power of your God-consciousness. It comes from the realization and acceptance of your True-self (God) manifested within the Earth Plane. Courage can only come from God, for God is the Creative Force….and in order to unite with courage to face that which blocks creativity you must be within your God-consciousness. Every time you open your eyes to a new day you are exercising your courage. Every time you walk out of your home to be part of the world around you, to be exposed to other energies, you are exercising your courage. The degree of courage is measured by the power of your Spirit, for every Be-ING possesses courage just by the mere fact that he is a God Be-ING. The more powerful your Spirit the more powerful your courage; subsequently, the more powerful the Creative Force exists within you. Your creative ability can be measured by the courage you possess.

Within your Ego Perception, fear manifests when confronted with the idea of courage, because the Ego realizes that courage is needed to overcome fear and negativity; this creates more fear within the Ego which then blocks you from coming into a state of courage. There are many questions within your Be-ING about how to use courage, how to obtain it and what you must recognize within your own Be-ING in order to connect to the courage. We will answer your questions about courage and what it means, in truth.

Q. I have prayed for the courage I need to put my photography work out to the public. I feel that my prayers are being answered because

I now seem to have trust in doing so. I am wondering if one needs to trust, before one gains his courage.

As we have said before, courage comes from your God-self, and by praying for courage you are turning your fear over to God -- you are within the courage of your True self in this act. Courage is the willingness to be in the moment and to turn over all of your fears in order to come into your Creative Force. To trust in what manifests is to display courage, for when you have turned over the fear that blocks you, you are opening the crown Chakra to receive more Light--you are freeing your Mental Body from the pressures of the Ego perception, and you are lightening the Emotional Body. All of this creates a peace within your Be-ING….and this state of grace brings forth trust in what manifests….and this trusting permits you the courage to create your True Self.

Changing the perception is the work that you must do from within….and in order to do this work you must have the courage to pass through the pain and the darkness that you perceive through your Ego-self. Only through turning over the Ego's fears to your God-self can you create the courage within the Ego to go forward in this endeavor.

Q. Why does the Ego block courage?

The Ego energy of your Be-ING is preoccupied with fear, and because it is motivated through its fear it does not seek the courage to overcome the fear; rather, it <u>becomes</u> the fear and, therefore, indulges itself within this negativity. When a Be-ING is fearful he becomes absorbed in what he fears and he is preoccupied with the situation that is motivating him to isolate his emotions and his mental abilities. This meaning: that when you are in pain the focus is absorbed within the pain....there is no other energy visible to your Be-ING except the pain that is taking place within the Physical, Mental or Emotional Bodies. You cut off all of your power to heal because you become this pain....you talk about the pain, you are preoccupied with trying to find methods to eliminate the pain and you are constantly drawing other people into your pain.

The Ego operates in this way because there is no trusting in the power of the God-self to heal. Even when a Be-ING is aware that he has this power, his Ego blocks this awareness by escalating the situation and the pain worsens. That is how the Ego blocks courage....courage would be to simply focus the energy into the pain in order to dissolve it by the power of the Light within your God-self. In turning it over to your God-self, you assist your energy in focusing to move forward in spite of the pain....this is when courage is present.

The Ego is the coward that lacks true courage; it is the selfish part of your energy, for it is only concerned with the body. If the Ego feels the body is attractive and healthy it feels powerful and it creates out of that power a more focused existence; yet this existence is always surrounded by greed and serving of the body through the material world. Your God-self, however, is the part of your energy that rises above the entrapment of the material and possesses the courage to transform the Ego's perception. To transform the Ego is to display great courage within your God-consciousness, for the Ego is the child and demands constant attention....paying attention through your God- consciousness is a <u>positive</u> action.

It is when you pay attention through the Ego that you become trapped by the Ego's fear and obsessed in what the Ego is experiencing with the physical. The Ego cannot do anything but block your courage because it is selfish within a material perception....your God-self, however, is selfish within a positive perception, meaning the God-self is serving the One energy. So the word `selfish` takes on a new meaning; in other words, you serve the self (the Whole) -- not the material `Ego-self,` but your God-self, which in this serving is an alignment with your Higher-Consciousness.

Q. I believe that it takes courage to act in certain ways, to perform certain tasks that are distasteful, and/or to associate with certain people at particular times only because one feels it necessary for survival and not because it is one's desire to do so.

What you are speaking of here is the Ego's manipulation of energy and you are confusing courage with manipulation. It does not take courage to do something when fear of survival is motivating the action. It is the fear that creates your spending time with people for whom you do not care and you manipulate your energy to accept your fate to do so. You are not displaying courage here. You display courage when you dismiss yourself from where you do not desire to spend time. This takes courage. Why? Because you are giving up the material reward for the higher reward, the unseen reward of peace and balance in your own energy.

That is why it is difficult for Be-ings of the Earth Plane to see courage as a natural act. They believe you must `muster up` courage, you must manufacture it in some way. This is the Ego's manipulating your energy....for courage is a natural state of being. When you are within the true light of courage you are able to rise above the material security and come into the emotional security of your God-self.

The only reason the Ego perceives courage in the act of doing something that it does not desire to do is because it is dependent on other Be-ings for its own identity, and it seeks confirmation from without rather than from within. This is what manipulates your Ego into doing things that you do not want to do. Therefore, you must see this clearly: what you speak of is not courage it is the Ego's manipulation of your Be-ING. The Ego manipulates your perception in order for you to be able to do that which, in fact, you do not want to do. In order to find the courage to not do that which is out of alignment with your True nature, you must release the fear of your material survival that motivates the action.

Q. Does action/movement towards that which you desire create courage and eliminate fear, or do you first need the courage to eliminate fear in order to take action?

First, you must understand that courage is already in existence, meaning you possess it. It is hidden from you by your Ego's perception, and the fear of not having courage is what keeps you from movement towards that which you desire.... so when you <u>are</u> moving towards your truest desire you are taking action you are within the light of your courage. If you are conscious, you are able to acknowledge that your courage is what motivates you to this action. Either approach is correct. The confusion comes when the action does not fit the perception.

175

Example: If you believe you have no talent as an artist, even though you act towards becoming an artist through taking classes and physically drawing, such acts will not aid you in overcoming the belief (which has been created out of fear) that you are not an artist. No matter how you work towards your goal you cannot manifest it without the perception of being a gifted artist. You only serve to prove to yourself that you are not gifted by failing at whatever actions you take.

Success comes out of the belief system, how you see yourself is what you manifest....so you must not be in contradiction with your actions and beliefs. Again, this takes place because your Ego has a distorted perception of courage. It believes `I want to be an artist, I believe I am not an artist and, therefore, I must find the courage to take action towards becoming an artist.` In this statement the Ego is saying that it needs to manipulate your energy in order for you to do something that within your deepest heart you do not believe you can....and this manipulation creates the negativity, the failure, and the pain that many Be-ings experience within this perception. Know that courage is a natural state of being and the work is to align the perception with the action. Then you shall manifest what you desire, in Truth.

I shall give you an exercise, (visualization) to assist you in connecting to your courage: Begin by creating a doorway/ window to the courage that exists in every moment. Go to this doorway/window and open it. See yourself looking through this opening, put yourself out into the space beyond, and see energy whirling around in colors of red, orange and gold the colors of courage. Then breathe in these colors of courage, see them go through your nostrils and into your chest, see your chest illuminated in red, orange and gold. Follow these colors as they circulate throughout your whole body. Connect to the intensity of their energy and feel the power of your own courage. Then say out loud,

`I feel propelled to give action, form and reality to my beliefs, for I am the `Mani- fester` of this moment within creation.`

Do this to open your connection to the energy of courage that exists within your willingness to consciously participate in your own life. See this as an act of celebration, for it is so..........

ANNA'S THOUGHTS: COURAGE

We believe that we are able only at certain times to connect to our courage-other times unable to touch it. We liken it to a `magical potion` it is there or it disappears like magic. This is the belief of our Ego. ASTRA says, however, that courage is always available to us and that it is our Ego that blocks us from connecting to this courage which exists in every moment.

Because we believe that courage is an external, aggressive force to be called upon in the face of disaster or major physical threat, we never understand that courage is an ever-present, peaceful, internal force the silent force that lives within. This lack of understanding comes from the pain held in our Child-self. The belief system of our Ego creates us to behave as a fearless protector of our Inner-child. Our Ego feels a need to `muster up` courage that is aggressive enough to protect the child, believing that all pain comes from the outside world. For this reason our ego may manifest in extreme ways, such as, overly combatant, belligerent, *or even `holier-than-thou,` etc., We interpret this behavior as true courage, it is not!*

True Courage is accepting that all pain is created by the perception held within past experiences of the inner child, and not of the outside world. This acceptance allows the Ego to take full responsibility to heal the child of its false perceptions. Courage, in truth, is facing the darkness within and taking responsibility for our pain. To take responsibility we must <u>accept</u> that which exists in the moment, the path of least resistance. Only through this path can we find the courage to confront our fears. Courage manifests out of love for self, which in turn creates acceptance of our True-self and others.

CHAPTER X
KARMA (REINCARNATION)

We have heard the Guardian Angel (ASTRA) refer to Karma many times in describing our pain, fear, and imbalances; and many of us have heard the expression, `it's my Karma,` or `that's Karma,` referring usually to a negative event or circumstance that befalls a person.

What exactly is Karma? Within our Ego, we have great difficulty believing in the concept of Karma, especially here in the Western world where we have been taught through our religious backgrounds that there is only one life, one chance to be good, to be perfect; and if we do not succeed, we are damned; yet if we please God, we are saved.

The pressure put upon us because of the belief in a singular life is so overwhelming that the Ego works to create more powerful illusions in order to protect itself from damnation (death). Fear and manipulation is created by the Ego because underlying everything that we do there is a deep belief in <u>Hell</u> and in not being perfect, in not reaching the state of purity that we believe God demands. The Ego's power in this illusion is supported through our religious beliefs in the singular life.

If we examine, however, the belief in Karma that exists in the Eastern philosophy, we see within it the opportunity to create more humility and acceptance. This is because belief in reincarnation offers numerous opportunities to discover the Self (God), to restructure and create a more peaceful, joyful, productive life. There is flexibility in this belief which we lack within all other beliefs.

We need to understand how our energy connects to the One Energy (God), and a true knowledge of Karma will guide us to this understanding. Most of us have a misconception of what Karma means. We see it as a pay-back for negativity created in this lifetime. Even when a positive outcome is seen as Karma, it is still viewed as pay- back, a reward for good behavior.

We asked ASTRA to explain the true meaning of Karma and our connection to its energy.

*Karma, in truth, speaks to cause and effect. It speaks to creating manifestations through the belief system. When a belief is within fear, it causes a Be-ING to act out his fears; and in so doing, he affects a negative manifestation of the particular fear that he holds. Therefore, every Be-ING within his life is manifesting through his belief system, through his perception; and in his manifestation he is either creating illusion or truth.

Because you are within Ego perception, the ability to manifest truth is limited; therefore, discovery of your True self cannot be accomplished within the limitations of one lifetime, one existence within Physical Body....for within one lifetime you are focusing in a small area, in that you are confined to circumstances that have been created to sustain the direction of the particular lifetime. This does not mean that enlightenment cannot be reached within one lifetime. What it means is that the design of the energy in the Whole follows a pattern, a law that sustains balance....and this law of cause and effect is always followed, for if it did not exist one would become lost in eternal darkness, illusion....so to understand what Karma is, you must begin to see that it is a tool for the learning of your True self--it is a powerful manifestation of cause and effect!

You have a saying that what you do comes around to meet you at some later point within your life. You say, `What goes around comes around.` This is meaning that you are always to face your own creations. Whatever you create you must confront. Confronting your creation is the opportunity to reach your God-self and put in balance that which was created out of the Ego perception. Only the Ego creates Karma, for the Ego is focused in the negative forces (in fear). God, meaning your God-self, possesses no Karma, for within your God-self all the laws of the universe are obeyed, understood, and cherished....so negativity and illusion are not manifested through this Higher- Consciousness.

The great pain that man suffers within the Earth because of this illusion of one lifetime, (one physical manifestation that you hold through your Ego perception) is the power that creates more limitation and darkness. If the Ego were to believe in reincarnation, then it would have to release its separateness from the One (God), it would have to accept that it is an energy which is eternally connected to God. This is why it is so difficult for the Ego to accept reincarnation as a reality. Remember, your Ego is hiding from Truth, from God, so it hides in the belief that there is only one life and that within this life it needs to suck out all of the joy, the power, the material, and physical manifestations because within the Ego's perception of life, there is only this <u>one</u> opportunity to `live.`

This is the part of your Be-ING that is desperate to escape the reality of your God-self….this is the part of your Be-ING that manifests the negativity within your Plane and keeps you spinning on the wheel of Karma….for this part of your Be-ING is forever creating decay of the physical. It cannot decay the One, for the cause and effect protects the One, meaning that as the Ego creates physical decay it is always facing its creation….it is always returning to relive and re-experience the negativity, the fear, the destruction that it has created until it arrives at an awakening through this repetition….an awakening that manifests its connection to the God-self which assists in creating balance out of this negative manifestation. That is your path, to create balance in all of the energy that your Ego distorted, and in so doing return you as Whole into the arms of the One (God).

There are many paths to God; so when you see a Be-ING who is on a path of self- destruction, for example, know that the experiencing of his creations of destruction is a path to his awakening….for he shall return lifetime after lifetime to face his creation of destruction until an awakening takes place within his Be-ING that gives him the power to balance his energy and sends him into the Light. Within the Light balance then can be created….and this Be-ING (this energy) can elevate to a new level of understanding the Self.

When you are open to this universal law of cause and effect which assists in balancing Karma, then you are able to accept reincarnation into your consciousness. In accepting, your arming your whole energy with the Light, the Power of God…. in so doing, you give to yourself a greater understanding of the Light that you possess from within….now you can see more clearly that this life you are within has great value in, that, it is here in order for you to learn and to grow into a Higher Consciousness. You are able then to value all that happens within this life, you are able to take the teachings that have come before and see the value of bringing in the Light in order to balance the negative energy which causes pain, suffering and decay within your Be-ING. You then can accept that you hold the power, that you are the Creator of your own existence within the Physical Plane….and you can trust in your eternal energy that you are forever in movement….experiencing your Whole-self and the Whole of creation.

Trusting allows you to see that there is no real limitation on your energy, that you are limitless, in truth, and, that you are focusing the Light of consciousness in a point in time….and it is called the physical embodiment. You are not just this point in time; you are all that exists and at the same instant you have given over all of the focus of the `One` into this point in time in order to experience the creation in an intimate manner…. in order to balance your chosen Karma through the senses of the Physical Body. This is a great gift that the God within you has given you for, in truth; you are joyful energy creating your own healing so you may return to the peace within, which is the limitless mind of God.

Q. If we are God-manifested, why did we in our beginning allow the Ego to fall out of alignment and create Karma?

First, you must remember that it was your unconscious state that created the `fall.` You must see that your Ego fell into a sleep-state, you did not have consciousness; therefore, it was not that you allowed this to happen it was created out of sleep.

Coming into the dense plane of the Earth, working with the Whole (the God-self) to create physical manifestations is what captured your energy. This is meaning, as we have said before, when you are captured by a thought or experience you shut down all of the other energies that exist, for your attention becomes absorbed in that thought or experience. In the same way, when you became captured by your own manifestations you shut down all of the energy that you are, in Truth, creating a sleep-state within your Ego and thereby its fall into illusion.

Q. Why are Karma and reincarnation not mentioned in the Old and New Testaments of the Bible?

At the beginning of your physical embodiment you were aware of your Karma and the reincarnation process through your religious teachings. It was discussed among the people of the Old Testament, they were basing their behavior on this information. It is what created the moral consciousness of the time of the religious Orthodox Israelites.

This knowledge was passed on and found its way to the New Testament through Jesus Christ. It was spoken of as Jesus told of his parables....HE spoke of returning, HE spoke of facing your creations, HE spoke of the Kingdom of Heaven that lives within and without. `HE` spoke of the cycles through which man passes. Many of his teachings have been misinterpreted; and most importantly, the Ego perception of man at this time took hold of the truth of that time and chose to eliminate from the Holy Scriptures all reference to Karma and Reincarnation for the purpose of controlling the people. This was influenced by an Ego Be-ING in power, a royal Be-ING of the time. The Church was forced to align with these ruling forces and saw an opportunity, through its Ego perception, to control the masses as well….for there was a belief that if the masses were fearful enough of God's wrath coming down upon them and of being burned in hell for eternity, that the Church then would have complete and total control, for it would have removed the power from man in his wisdom of reincarnation and would have empowered itself, as an institution to accumulate wealth, property and influence over the physical world. This outcome created a distortion that has led man down a path of deep confusion and lack of love for self.

Q. Is the purpose of reincarnation to grant us the opportunity to balance our Karma, and do we choose our identities and circumstances prior to each lifetime?

This is the purpose of reincarnation - to balance Karma. Reincarnation was created out of your Higher-self when the Ego fell out of alignment. It was created as a tool in assisting your Ego-consciousness to realign with the God-consciousness. Falling out of alignment is what manifested separation from the Whole, creating fear and all dense and dark manifestation, which is, in truth, illusion, for it is not in alignment with the Creative Force…here is the great design of your God-self, giving the Ego multitudes of opportunity to awaken and realign with the Whole. Therefore, when you are preparing to come into body, you are preparing to work on balancing past Karmic experiences, and you, in connection with your God-self, create the circumstance of your birth…. meaning that choices are created which support the lesson, the Karma, that is in need of balance.

Example: When a Be-ING creates Karma by living a lifetime as the subject of abuse (turning over his power to the abuser and falling into the negativity that the experience creates), he will continue to repeat the experience in future lives until he balances the experience by coming into the Light of his God-self; therefore, he will choose circumstances within the present life which allow him to face the abuse once more in order to release the Karma created out of the original experience. He will choose, along with the abuse, certain strengths that he has acquired from past lives....for each time the Be-ING faces the same Karma, he adds new elements to assist him with this balance. He brings in Be-ings from past lifetimes who had created in him an awakening and who now would assist him with his negative perception. He also brings in wisdom acquired in his Emotional and Mental Bodies. Everything is designed by your God-self, directed through your Spiritual guides to assist you in balancing your Karma within the Physical Plane.

Q. Are all relationships Karmic?

First, we will say that all Karma comes out of Ego perception, for the perception of the Ego is what creates the dense experience in which your energy becomes trapped. The entrapment is the Karma. When you are within God-consciousness your energy continues to flow and there is no entrapment; therefore, no Karma.

Within relationships, Karma is created when the relationship is perceived through Ego, when there are past Ego experiences trapped within a Karmic interaction. There are relationships within the Light, as well, which are created out of your God-consciousness. These relationships are of growth, for they are focused in movement, meaning the learning and releasing of Ego perception, and Ego desire, always conscious of the Light within and the love that guides their existence.

You see here, there are Karmic relationships and there are Godly relationships. Through the Godly relationship you grow in wisdom and that wisdom is directed into a future life to assist you in balancing your Karma.

Q. You have taught us that our Ego mind is in control of the Earth Plane. Does that mean that our thoughts, feelings and all perception are karmic?

Karma is the manifestation created out of your Ego perception. Your thoughts are not karmic they are thoughts, meaning that they are endless possibilities in mind. They become karmic when the Ego directs the energy from the thought into manifestation. If the thought were directed through your God-consciousness it would manifest on a high plane; therefore, there would be no karmic repercussions.

Your feelings are the same they are feelings. Feelings exist within the physical. In order to have meaning, they must be interpreted through the Emotional Body. When your Ego interprets the feeling, it creates an action and that action creates a reaction, this is Karma. It is not Karma when your feelings are interpreted through your God-consciousness. So you must see here that it is the cause and effect through the Ego perception that manifests your Karma and it is the balancing energy of your God perception that releases the Karma and frees your energy so it may continue in its reuniting with the Creator (God).

Q. When a person feels a strong connection to a country or culture of which he has no present knowledge, is it from past lifetimes?

This is correct, for when a Be-ING has a strong connection to a language, for example, it is easy for him to learn this language it flows through his consciousness because he has spoken it before. When he feels familiar with a culture other than the one in which he lives and he has the opportunity to experience that culture in this life, he will immediately recognize the culture as being something personal to his own energy, knowing on a deeper level that he has lived this culture before.

When you come into a life, you hold the memory of the lifetime in which the Karma that you are working on in this lifetime existed. That is why the memory of the culture, the language and the country are extremely appealing to your present self....because there are traces of memory within your cellular structure that came with the Karma into this life. Remember, you are working on balancing a specific Karma in each lifetime, so all memory comes with the cells within your Be-ING from the lifetime in which you originated the particular Karma. That is why when you feel familiar with something or someone of which you have no personal knowledge in the present lifetime, you are experiencing a past life connection.

Q. If a person has a strong pull toward a certain profession or service, is this due to Karma?

It is Karma coming from past only when the desire for the service or profession is overwhelming and there is a deep obsession with this goal; then it is your destiny you cannot avoid its manifestation because you have created all the necessary elements to ensure you're experiencing this service or profession, for this is where your Karma lies….so if a Be-ING is not sure of what he desires to do in life and he floats from one position to another he is exploring himself in order to find direction. This is not a karmic experience because it is free choice that he is exploring. This means his Karma is not focused in his service and/or profession.

Q. How is a person with a criminal mind who is seemingly without conscience served by his Karma to come into the Light?

Be-ings have difficulty in accepting that a negative event is within truth, but you must understand that you, as a God Be-ING within the dense energy of the Earth, are here to explore the positive and negative vibrations you experience in order to create balance; therefore, to experience the negative assists you in creating balance with the positive, for when a Be-ING is a criminal in this lifetime he is working with the Ego and Karma that he has created in many past lifetimes. He is absorbed within Ego perception and the God-self is blocked from his consciousness. He will experience the devastation of the Ego and its consequences which will create the desire of peace to rise up within his Be-ING. As it begins to rise, he shall begin to search; and in his searching he will see, at first, glimpses of Light that he will follow from lifetime to lifetime until he has created a balance with the positive and negative within.

Every Be-ING is served through his God-self. Every Be-ING brings to himself…. exactly what is needed within each moment. If he needs more pain and devastation through his Ego perception, he shall receive it, for in receiving it he is served. He suffers the darkness from within and this pain and suffering will ultimately awaken him. Be-ings in the Earth Plane judge what they do not understand, for those who are more in balance with the positive energy become frustrated with those who are not. This is because they, themselves, are not completely within the Light; therefore, they cannot see the wisdom that is within the negative forces in the Earth Plane. You must remember that the Earth is the school of learning. It is the place in which you balance your Karma as you raise your vibration in order to align yourself with the Light (God).

Q. What about the innocent victims of crime? Can you explain how Karma operates in their life?

First, you must remember that there are no victims! This is a perception of the Ego. In Truth, everything that takes place manifests because you have created its manifestation, for you are the Creator within the Earth Plane. When a Be-ING is killed when he is attacked by another, there are many experiences from past that have created this happening. As Spirit, you work and prepare to come into Physical Body for the purpose of balancing the energy (Karma). This means that many souls accept in playing the role of what you call a `victim` in order to serve the balancing of Karma. There are multitudes of reasons that create a manifestation.

Example: If a child dies, many times the death is to serve the Karma of the parent, for the parent is balancing a Karma with loss, abuse, or an emotional separation; and this child (meaning this soul) is assisting in the lesson, for the death creates an awakening within the parent which directs his energy toward a greater understanding in the area in which he is working with his Karma.

There are Be-ings who have abused others in past lifetimes and who are now working to experience their own abuse in order to create an understanding of their Karma and, therefore, balance the perception by bringing the abuse into the Light. This is meaning: that in future lives the Be-ING will be free of this Karma and will not repeat the abuse of the past.

There are many, many scenarios created to serve in the raising of man's consciousness in order to unite with his True-self. Every Be-ING will serve the positive and the negative throughout his many incarnations. He will play many roles in order to release the Karma and to see the Truth and to rise to the level of the Creator (God).

Seeing this Truth enables you to work within the moment within this lifetime....to create balance from within, to discover the Karma that you hold, and to work in releasing the grip it has upon your Be-ING. The gift of knowing your own power enables you to change from a Be-ING in darkness and fear to a Be-ING within Light and Love <u>in an instant</u>.

Q. Does the law of Karma deny my free will?

You are not denied your free will, for your free will guides you in balancing your Karma. Karma is a manifestation of negativity and distortion in the perception of past experiences. Free will is what you use in order to direct your energy in discovering where you are blocked in your perception, and how to create balance within your own Be-ING, and your own experiences in the present manifested life.

191

Also destiny in that which is destined to happen exists. There are situations which are destined, but your free will created them....before you came into Body, your free will had created what was destined in order to assist you with the Karma that you chose to balance in this life. Example: You might choose a specific profession to which you are destined because your Karma lies within that situation and recreating it is needed to balance the Karma....so understand clearly, free will is yours because you are the Creator (God), you are a manifestation of the One; therefore, you are unlimited!

Q. If all people of the Earth were to align their Egos and come into God-Consciousness, would that eliminate Karma and the need to reincarnate? Would the Earth still exist?

If all the Be-ings of the Earth Plane were within Higher-consciousness, there would be no Karma. There would remain free choice and the unlimited mind of God; therefore, reincarnating would continue only, if there were a desire to take physical form. The purpose of the Earth would elevate. It would no longer be a school for balancing Karma. It would become a Heavenly manifestation (a paradise), for it would be directed through the God-consciousness and there would be only love and joy in the hearts and minds of all who occupy the Earth. Such an experience is an elevated one that your energies are destined to create and explore.

The Earth, itself, is working to reunite man to the Truth.... for if man does not come into his Higher-consciousness, the negativity that already weighs heavy on the Planet Earth will grow more.... dense. The Earth cannot hold the gravity of such dense energy and, therefore, it will pass through many physical changes. Much destruction will take place, many lives will be lost through this devastation, and your God-self (the God from within and the God from without) will release once more the darkness that was created (and which is consuming the Light) and begin again.

Q. May we please have a guided meditation that will assist us in coming into our `Higher Consciousness?`

To be aware of the energy that composes your Whole Be-ING, to be within consciousness in every moment is to direct your attention from within, knowing that all that is manifested is manifested through your perception; for that which you perceive is the Creator of the material world. Knowing your power and how great that power is, in Truth, is the key to releasing yourself from the illusions created out of the dense energy within the Ego....to know that you are a reflection of the One....to remember that you are not your Body, you are not only the physical forms that you experience within the Earth, but that you are also the energy that is outside of the physical creation.

The entrapment that you experience in the Earth Plane is an illusion that limits your power, limits your wisdom, and limits your joy....for to be unlimited, you must connect to the power of mind and direct that power into the Light....not into the darkness, the fear, the judgments and the pain which create physical decay, but into the Light where there is always a continuous `re-birthing` taking place within your energy.

All the levels of your Be-ING, when in unison with the Creation, provide a freedom from the density and the gravity of the Physical Plane. You are this unlimited energy, you are a manifestation of the One (God) ....and within your Be-ING you hold all of creation within the cells, within the mind, the heart and the Spirit....you are a reflection of the eternal energy, the Spirit of God; therefore, meditate on this Truth and allow it to work through you and for you, so you may be the perfect reflection of joy and of love manifested within the Earth Plane.

Trusting that you are not alone in this life, that you are being guided from the Angelic- Realm, the Angels that have been assigned to your energy before you came into body will help you greatly to let go of the fear and hopelessness that was created through the Ego perception.

Duality exists in the Earth experience. Duality creates conflict with the God-self.... for the God-self is all inclusive.... there is no duality in God! Through meditation you release the Earth Plane and its duality, through meditation you connect to your God-self.

Knowing who you are that you are (One) with God, you are freed from the duality. Directing your mind to see the world as it is in Truth (all inclusive) you no longer live in the conflict of duality: rather you are the True Creator an extension of God on the Earth Plane.

In your meditation see the Light, see it as a waterfall of White Light.... see it very bright and very white. Follow the waterfall of Light as it passes over stars and planets and see that the stars and planets are illuminated in the Light. Follow as the Light illuminates the vast darkness in the Universe. All is seen in the Light nothing is hidden. Continue to follow the Light as it washes over the Earth and then penetrates the Earth and fills it from within. Now see yourself....see the waterfall of White Light wash over your body....see the Light penetrate your body through the `Crown-Chakra` and visualize the Light filling you from within. Know that you are the Light and then ask from your heart and you shall receive.

Remember that you are blessed and you are guided. Remember you do not walk alone....you walk with multitudes in the Light of the `ONE.`

My Eternal Love, the Guardian Angel (ASTRA)

LIVING AT ATTENTION SYNOPSIS - ASTRA'S TEACHINGS

Anna Speaks:

All the information from the Angelic Realm is an eternal ongoing effort to teach mankind of his powerful role within the creation. It is presented here by ASTRA for the purpose of aiding humanity in raising the consciousness, in order to save the planet Earth and to insure the continuation of the human race.

The teachings begin by expressing an important fact, which is, that we humans live in sleep-state and this is why we no longer are capable of recognizing what is Truth. Distraction from the truth comes in the form of materializing our greed; by focusing all our efforts to gain power through possessing wealth believing that the material is the only valuable way to live and to survive in our world.

ASTRA shows us the error in this thinking, while describing the True path to realizing how powerful we `truly` are when we are living to serve the Creation. Through our service, we begin to recognize that we are all, `One` energy which connects us to our fellowman. Although we express ourselves in multitudes of ways that differ from each other the core of our being is the same. For we all desire to experience love and peace, comfort and stability....that will come through the manner in which we have chosen to live our lives.*

ASTRA shows us that our Ego is what blocks our true instincts through our attachment to fear and illusion, which is the creator of all our <u>negative</u> emotions. Our sleep-state is created out of these false emotions. Fear/illusion is what keeps us from seeing the Truth which exists in our world, in our personal life, collective life, (mass consciousness). Every person in creation is seeking the truth about him/herself for every person craves peace, love and joy, knowing intuitively that these emotions are what sustain us in all areas of our life. We are all seeking the truth whether consciously or unconsciously, for Truth is the eternal energy which drives everything we experience on this planet. Therefore, it is our loving obligation to come into <u>Truth</u> and erase all <u>illusion</u> from our consciousness.

At this time in our world we are experiencing living in chaos and we fear what we do not understand. When we fear the negative events going on around us, this fear creates a negative Mass-consciousness. Therefore, in order to protect us from what we fear and see as negative; we work to <u>eliminate</u> all that we fear....and do not understand. Without consciousness of our True value and Personal power we will be destroyed by our own ignorance of self! Now is the moment to show a new path, a new direction, a new consciousness for healing the whole self....mind, body, and spirit.

Through man's exploration of the total self a new consciousness emerges, the Higher-self.

Following our instincts and opening to our `Higher` consciousness is "<u>following the better angels of our nature</u>." These words were spoken by Abraham Lincoln in his speech on `The duty of a Statesman.` Surely Abraham Lincoln was speaking about being at a State of Attention when he first spoke these words; for our being in this state of attention creates a positive awareness that keeps and protects our energy from sleep- state (danger). Following a deep inner knowing is receiving God/Truth into our heart (the Center of our being) where our True nature resides (`better angels`).

Living at attention strengthens our ability to know; for it brings us the messages that tell us what to do and how to respond in all situations. When we are living at attention we are than in a wakeful state. We create our existence through utilizing our whole self (mind, body, and spirit). This is what increases our ability to do our work well for through an awakened state we are within Total consciousness. Consciousness provides the greatest protection from all that is harmful in our world, for it provides creativity for solving the problems we face within our earthly life. The teachings from ASTRA are a loving gift to us which provides the guidance that awakens us to this Truth.

The conclusion: We are the Creator manifested in physical body. We are the healers of our own life and the love that we hold for the Creation/Creator is than now equal to the love that we hold for ourselves.

Chapter XI
Selective Moments--
ASTRA's Personal Guidance

September 20, 2001
New York City Private Channel

ASTRA: We are here, you are welcomed. You are to speak.

Woman: *I've been very upset and shaken by the recent attacks that have happened on NY City which is where I live, as well as in Washington.... and I'm very afraid that this will lead us into the next world war from which the earth may never recover or we may not even survive the planet. I was hoping to get some guidance from you ASTRA, as to how I can move beyond this fear and what I can do to help lift the earth higher.*

ASTRA: Love is the healer. Love is what lifts the earth for love is what God is. Therefore, fear and love cannot exist together. Where there is fear there cannot be love. Where there is love there cannot be fear. So man must choose between fear and love. This is very difficult for man at this moment because he is consumed with anger. Fear and anger are companions....they are opposite sides of one energy.

Man in the physical plane is asleep so, therefore, he is ignorant of what has manifested in truth. The ego believes that everything that takes place, takes place OUTSIDE of him (in other words), man through his ego believes everything is happening to him from without. Coming at him from without....and this is an illusion. **Everything manifests from your center, which is meaning that man brought this upon himself.**

Man as a collective energy brought this negativity up into the consciousness, into the Mass consciousness, and why did he do this? Because the earth cannot sustain this negativity, the earth cannot sustain this darkness, this hatred, this prejudice, that man in mass energy (consciousness) has created on the earth plane. This negative creation isn't only of this time there have been multitudes of lifetimes creating this darkness. Man creates it and then escapes it, by denying that it belongs to him. Denying that he is part of it he does his good deeds to cover it over and now it has exploded in his face. HE has exploded it, because MAN is not only ego he is also God-consciousness and the God within man recognizes that unless he faces his darkness and heals himself, the earth will perish man will perish, therefore, man brought this to himself in order to heal.

Now it is difficult for Be-ings on the physical plane to recognize this.... to see the truth in it, because in your physical world you live in duality therefore, you see the good people, the bad people, the right people, and wrong people. You view everything in a `dualistic` manner; you see things as either right or wrong and in this perception you are in the illusion, **for the truth is that all is `One energy` (God).** All is the Creator so all is inclusive. There is no separation. There is no duality in the kingdom of the Creator therefore; your belief in duality is an illusion.

We are not saying that because the earth is an illusion that it means this is bad or wasteful. We speak of it as an illusion that is helping man to work in balancing his karma; where man works to recognize the darkness and balance it with the Light. The illusion was created through Ego and man has lost his way, he has fallen asleep and separated from his spiritual self; which holds all wisdom, and now man is left believing in the illusion alone as his reality, **this belief is what will destroy the creation of the Earth**. Therefore, through the mass consciousness the God-self within each Be-ING has taken charge and brought all of the negativity to an eruption, in order to place the Truth into the consciousness of man and assist him in his awakening.

What you must recognize is that you are not the good guys or the bad guys you are both. The Be-ings that attacked you are also both and you are each out of balance and, therefore, you are both needing to reach a balance. This will not be simple for there is so much illusion in your plane that even as you work to correct this, (to make a correction) you will be tempted to fall back into sleep as soon as it all dies down and there is not much talk of it only the structural building and the cleaning up evidence of your pain.

As man begins to fall back into sleep man will be continuously bringing to himself more disastrous events in order to re-awaken. There will be more events in order for man to stay awake. If man does not stay awake (live in a wakeful state), he will not be able to make the corrections that need to be made. What are the corrections we speak of? They are to expose the darkness and bring love for healing into the present existence of darkness, transforming the darkness into Light, lifting the consciousness of the Earth.

Man has become most especially in America a material worshiper, meaning God has become immaterial. Man has isolated himself in this materialism and he no longer remembers how to connect to other Be-ings through his heart. He no longer knows how to share himself, his love, nor his resources, with his neighbor. He is on a constant road of accumulation for himself. This is depicting the fear that the ego possesses in each Be-ING; the fear of poverty, the fear of death, the fear of loss of freedom, to move about freely in his world. Man no longer fully trusts his instincts man no longer trusts his heart, man no longer trusts that his `True joy' comes from <u>service</u> to his fellow man.

You can see this very clearly after this disaster for man began to open his heart, began to serve one another and began to feel the joy of that service, feeling in these moments his True identity....Love and Compassion, Humility within Service to his fellow man.

Man must ask himself why does it take a disaster to bring out his God-self, `True identity.` Why in times of peace does he hide like a frightened child behind the material forces rather than serve through his instincts. Why does he give his power over to his government, to his fear of loss, to his portfolio, to the so called expert, when HE can only be the TRUE expert concerning his own `LIFE.` When he does this he is not taking responsibility for himself for he is not recognizing his True power. Man's power lies in Service, the power lies in Love, the power lies in Sharing and opening your borders wider and wider in order to understand yourself and others. Only then can you truly share yourself within humanity.

This lesson will come hard for the human race and there will be many, many Be- ings that will stay in their sleep-state, but there shall also be many, many who shall <u>awaken</u> and they shall become the beacons of Light that will magnetize all those who are searching....and their numbers will grow stronger and stronger yet, this will not take place in an instant, for you did not create all of this negativity greed and separation, in an instant. It took multitudes of lifetimes to do so. We are not saying it will take multitudes of lifetimes to undo it, we are saying, that it will take as long as it takes to get many Be-ings to <u>awaken</u> to this truth, and when there are many your world will change and you will restructure all of the institutions that you have created through Ego-consciousness....you will create them through your God-consciousness and you will create a world that is balanced, where there is freedom not only in America but all over the Earth. Abundance will exist everywhere and the sharing of knowledge, wisdom, and abundance, will take place on your entire planet. You will not need to be policed than by great governments or legal systems....for you will police yourselves and they will exist <u>only</u> as overseers. What is said here sounds like (to a man or woman in Ego-consciousness) a dream that can never be and will never be. `**Dreams are the realities that AWAKEN through conscious action.**`

There is a cleansing of your Earth taking place it is beginning now. Those who need to leave New York shall leave and those who stay need to change the past painful moments through many aggressive actions of love. What the individual Be-ING needs to do is to release the fear through understanding the purpose of what has happened from the depth of his Be-ING. Accepting his/her responsibility to heal the SELF, every Be-

ING must work through his Center releasing his/her own fears, bringing all of his/her darkness into the consciousness--just as what has happened in this tragedy that the darkness was hidden and through this act has now come up into the Mass-consciousness. Each Be-ING must bring his/her individual darkness up into his/her own consciousness in order to <u>awaken</u> and heal the Self.

Where you will then be is free to serve without being burdened by fear of loss, whether it is physical, mental, material, or spiritual, that you will no longer fear. For when you are in God-consciousness you know you can never lose-because you are one with the CREATOR and whatever manifests in physical form is there for a purpose, which is perhaps beyond your physical comprehension. The not knowing works only because you know that you never ever lose your connection with the `One` for you are the `One.`

These are very high minded concepts that many Be-ings cannot come close to understanding, yet, every Be-ING is being challenged now to work in this direction. Some will come a great distance while others will come a fair distance, others will come a short distance. Those who are in doubt do not move at all and, therefore, will suffer great pain and confusion.

Any movement towards the Truth shall bring great power and more Light into the physical plane which will heal and elevate man through his darkness and into his/her `Higher` consciousness.

Woman: *So all the people who died in the recent attacks was it their time to leave the earth plane?*

ASTRA: They chose this before they came into body they chose to help in the healing of the planet. They chose to be in this position: in order to bring to the attention of all the souls on the earth the Truth-(about what is blocking the God Energy). They before they came into body chose to leave in this way in order to open that gate. They are blessed souls, every one of them are high souls, high energy, for they have chosen something of great sacrifice.

When you are in physical body you are enjoying the Creation through the senses; you are intimate with the Creation as you cannot be in any other form. It is a sacrifice of great magnitude and it was chosen before these Be-ings came into body, therefore, the Be-ings that are on the other side of this tragedy also chose. They made the choice to give up their lives, they made the choice to create the terror that would erupt and awaken man and in this they are also blessed.

This is VERY difficult for you to accept. It is very difficult for any Be-ING in physical body, in Ego-consciousness, to understand. In order to understand it you would have to understand that you are all `One Energy.` You would have to understand that separation is an illusion. You would have to understand that within your physical structure you are the `Universe` not only the physical planet but the entire Creation. You are a microchip of the whole and you are the whole complex image that this statement is implying. It is your Ego that rejects this idea yet, I say to you it is so!

There are no demons here except ignorance through loss of memory. That is your demon and every Be-ING on the planet is responsible because every Be-ING is asleep and in loss of memory of his True self (`United Self`).

Woman: *Did the Be-ings that died, did they suffer or did their souls leave?*

ASTRA: Immediately and continuously their souls left. They suffered in the sense of fear, fear was the great suffering. Panic was the great suffering, yet many of them turned this over immediately, many of them, did NOT suffer great panic or fear. Many of these souls immediately when realizing that their life was ending turned themselves over to the Creator and went peacefully. There were very few that went in panic, trust what I tell you VERY FEW! Most surrendered in peace. Seeing the situation in an instant they said: "God, I am ready".… then their souls and Ether bodies left the physical and they went into the Light. Therefore, the physical body felt no pain or fear in the moment of dying.

These souls are now watching over the Earth plane as we speak they are all in the wisdom of what has happened and why. Each of them is sending MORE LOVE into the minds and hearts of the Be-ings on the Earth within this place of great sadness. Here is the reason why you see your government moving slowly and cautiously because although they do not acknowledge this…. they feel the guidance coming from the spirits that have left.

The angelic realms are guiding all Be-ings to feel the love and compassion for one another. Love is now HERE in your plane and in your hearts and you must let it continue by not allowing it to be blocked, for if blocked you shall fall back into sleep- state. Follow your mission: your mission is to keep LOVE alive.

Woman: *Is that what is at the core of this in all of those people who perpetrated the attacks? Is that where all the hatred comes from at their core, that they don't love themselves?*

ASTRA: Always where there is hatred there is no love. What happened was born out of misconception it comes from an illusion, it comes from moving in a state of sleep rather than a state of wakefulness. Man hates himself when he doesn't know himself. He doesn't know who he is in Truth, he believes he is the duality that he lives in, he believes he is what he is taught from other Be-ings who are also lost in that duality, therefore, he believes his darkness must be hidden from the world, (for self- protection). When he hides his darkness (his hatred of self) it takes over and controls his existence and he lives in constant pain, conflict, and separation. This is what perpetuates the darkness in everything that he does and he falls deeper and deeper into sleep-state. Hatred stems from not sharing yourself with others, from hiding your darkness and believing that you are alone in your negative feelings of self. When in truth all Be-ings are both dark and `Light`…. both exist in your plane of duality. Face your darkness and you will gain the power to embrace your Light and live in joy.

Woman: *At this moment are there many people on this planet living within their own Separate Realities?*

ASTRA: That is correct. Each individual has his own form of reality yet there are masses of realities that are joined. In other words, there are masses of people that live under one reality and that reality is an illusion no matter what reality you are looking at on the physical plane it is all an illusion. It is not real even when you see something and you say, "O, there exists a good reality here in America," it is still an illusion for you do not have control of your life in America in truth (not in totality), although it looks like a good reality and works better than other realities; where people are starving and have no freedom of movement. This is true! The illusion you share in America is much healthier and happier than the darker illusions people live within some other countries. It is the mass belief system; created by the `Entities` in control in all countries which create the illusions -- `MASS realities` that you experience in your world. It is always man who corrupts through a lack of True consciousness; therefore, you are now experiencing the mass Ego-consciousness in your physical world.

There exists also an individual reality that man creates for himself, his own hidden belief system which directs his personal life. This means the personal belief system (the one that you hold for yourself) either creates your life as a hell or a heaven. You are the creator of heaven and hell through your own personal belief system. That is why two Be-ings can be in the same place, and ONE can perceive it as the place that has no negative effect on him; a place that does not rule his life, a place where he can rise above what is taking place and create his own peace and joy. The OTHER person sees it as a struggle and is constantly trying to be accepted by that which is outside of him....seeing life as a struggle and as a dark place there is no joy (it is a joyless life). His struggle creates his personal reality to reflect the mass-consciousness; for his individual perception of struggle further creates his existence within that mass- consciousness.

This is meaning you are all here to RISE above the illusion and create your TRUE reality. A reality that is shared which is established on the `Higher` consciousness. Then Earth will become a heaven and man/woman will achieve his/her divine birth right, Peace and Joy.

What makes America powerful and prosperous? America was created from your entire planet. The many diversified people that call America their home are a combination of all the cultures that exist on the Planet Earth. This is what creates the balance which serves a wide range of wisdom and thought processes. Interaction with diversified qualities possessed by humans of different cultures, creates combinations of energy which has the power to raise the intelligence and wisdom of the human race.

Remember that the True-self is the God-self and you are all `One` in this SELF.

Allow yourself to absorb what has been given in this time and open your heart to receive guidance from your `Higher-self.` Go now in peace.

ASTRA

MAY 16, 2001
ANGELIC GROUP CHANNEL
DREAMING— ASTRAL PLANE

ASTRA: All is <u>here</u>. All that exists is here, existing within this moment, for all that is within this moment is all that exists within the Creation. Everything that you can imagine or know is known within the `consciousness` of the moment. Therefore, all illusion falls away when man is focused within the moment, when the mind and the heart are focused in that which exists in the now. Then there is no room for that which is an illusion of the past, or fantasy of the future, and all that is remaining is the `Living Moment.`

For man to live in the moment is very difficult. This is because man is conditioned by the Ego-consciousness to live only in the illusion. This is meaning that the mind is constantly moving, constantly thinking constantly creating fear. Therefore, man works to rearrange his thoughts in order to change that which he fears is the truth within the moment. This act shows clearly that you are not living in the moment, but rather you are in the illusion. How is this so? If you were in the `living moment,` then your mind would be at rest and fear would not control. When the mind is at rest it is alert and open to receive all the wisdom held in the moment. When the mind is open to receive the `Living Moment,` the mind is no longer in ego fear....but rather in God (Truth).

All of you here have lived multitudes of lifetimes just within the physical Earth Plane itself. Through each embodiment you became wiser in many ways, although you are not conscious of this truth; it is the experience of life in body which brings you closer and closer to the `Living Moment.` Be confident of this fact and embrace it by asking questions that will further your education of the Self.

Q. When we ask for protection from God and the angels, when we are driving for example, can you tell us how this is handled and are there times when the help is withheld?

ASTRA: Nothing is ever withheld from the God force. If it is blocked, it is blocked through your own energy. You have the power through the ego to block out the God energy. Now this sounds like a contradiction, but it is not, for you have been told that God is all there is and that God is the only True power…. and this is so! Yet, in this dense plane of the Ego you have lost the memory of this truth….and without the memory of the Truth you live within a false reality which then becomes your Truth.

This is how powerful you are….because you are `One` with the God energy (the Creator), your power is great. Yet, (at the same time) in this physical embodiment you are in loss of memory. Therefore, you follow a false truth through your created Ego-consciousness. Now you believe in the `material consciousness` through your Ego, and this belief is what blocks you from God, True consciousness.

Understand that this is why you do not see everyone bringing in the Light and calling the Angels for protection when in their cars. You can only utilize what you know and deeply believe in-where there is true awareness. Here is the reason you block the protection you ask for, how can you call in that which you think you believe in, that which you are not sure you believe in…. how can you ask only through fear of danger? The outcome in this way of thinking can only block the power from the angelic realm. Angels assist when they feel your love and trust in the God force. Now understand: when you are deeply connected to the love of your True self, you have access to the greatest power in all of creation (the Creator). Then you may ask in joy….and invite the angels to ride with you in your car, in order to keep you conscious and aware of any danger that might lie ahead. This does not mean that you are depending on the angels to create magic that would keep you from an accident or death, <u>no</u>, for magic is part of the illusion and the Creative Force works through Love, the True magic within Creation.

It is difficult for the Ego to accept outcome that would end its existence. Yet, outcome is the passage of energy that exists for continually making correction. In order to expand the Light, correction must be made. This is meaning: whatever the physical outcome is, it exists for creating balance. Therefore, if you are meant to die in a car accident it is because it is time for your energy to move into a higher balance. Staying conscious means you accept all outcomes through deep love and trust in the Creative force (your Eternal force).

Q. If everything happens in order to work for correction, what can we do when we're dreaming, to realize what the dream wants to tell us, or teach us?

ASTRA: Dreaming is very powerful; when you are dreaming your energy is focused in the `Astral` plane. You are focused in your Astral body and the dream state is the state in which you are assisted and guided in healing the self. Dreams help you recognize your True identity; you are witnessing in dream state past lives and/or present life. In the dream state you are being guided by your Spiritual body; your Spiritual body is guiding your energy to see (and to learn how) to recognize that which is blocking you in your present moment (awake state).

As you have read in the chapter on the Astral body, the dream is what shows you where you are in the moment concerning your everyday reality. Dreams highlight your fears and your resistance to change. When the dream is dark and confused it is displaying your deepest fears, fears that you have been experiencing over many lifetimes. Analyzing these dreams is important for understanding how your consciousness works when blocking and challenging moments occur which you now experience in your awake-state.

Dreams tell you what you need to understand about yourself-so you may change the way you confront situations in your life which now damage you and block your power.

Example: Dream

A lion is following you and you begin to run faster and faster to escape danger. Then, suddenly you stop in front of a house-opening the door and letting the lion in closing the door behind you. What does this dream show you?

This dream is describing your greatest fear, (power) that you are in fear of your own power. The lion represents power in the dream, and you are running away from it until you exhaust yourself. Then you decide to invite the power into your home which represents your Be-ING. The home in a dream is your unconscious; it is the Inner-self. This dream is showing you that you exhaust all other means of escape in undesirable situations, and only when you become drained of energy do you give into what exists. Here is the lesson that you need to learn: how to help yourself to change a destructive habit, a habit created through your fear of your power to confront life on its own terms.

All dreams when rightly interpreted have great messages for guiding you on your journey. Sometimes a dream will reveal a negative relationship in your life, a relationship that you are in where you depend on another person for companionship, love or protection, (or all the above). This dream is very difficult to accept when it is shown that this relationship is, in truth, damaging to your life.

Example: Dream

You are riding on a train and your partner is sitting next to you and is holding your hand. The train begins to move very fast-and you squeeze the hand of your partner. The partner then gets up and walks over to another person across the aisle-and takes their hand; then turns in the opposite direction and begins to walk to the back of the train with this other person. You get up to follow, but the train is moving too fast for you to keep your balance, and you fall to the floor. You are left crying on the floor of the train when it suddenly crashes.

This dream is saying that the train, which represents sexual movement, is showing- that the partner is moving quickly to another partner. When taking that person to the back of the train which represents going behind your back, the partner is seeing someone else in an intimate way. You're trying to follow represents that you know on an intuitive level that something is wrong. You are seeking to find out what is happening when you become overwhelmed with so much emotion that you cannot move, so you fall and crash to the floor. This is meaning: you are overcome with weakness, created through fear of confronting what you feel is happening, so you give in to your emotions and hurt yourself rather than confront the partner.

This dream is showing you that you are afraid to confront the other person-for fear that you will find out what you do not want to know. The dream seeks to teach you that knowing the truth will be far less painful and damaging than your fear of the truth. **Knowing the truth never damages you, rather it creates your True freedom**.

Many people are taught directly through their dreaming. Others are not aware of being taught and at the same time they are being guided to awaken to some fear-which works to keep them blocked in life. This means that one can be blocked by not trusting themselves to make the right decision in a situation that needs to be dealt with. It is fear of rejection, pain, suffering, losses, and feelings of abandonment, which are the `highest energies` that block trust (movement) in the physical plane.

Therefore, here is the reason why dreams can be very confusing and chaotic. Within these dreams lies the greatest fear one holds from their past lives and/or the present life. When these dreams appear, the inner work being done is very powerful, for it is a delicate operation that is taking place through the Spiritual body of the person dreaming. While you are extended within sleep in the physical you are dreaming from the `Astral` plane and the energies are being guided from the Angelic Realm (Spiritual body). This is where the angels work to create the inner healing that takes place (releasing of blocked energy from the body).

Many times through your dreaming, you are releasing past experiences which are now blocking your True consciousness. Even though you are not consciously aware that this is taking place, it is so. It takes many lifetimes to release the past hurtful, wrongful, negative experiences, which are keeping you prisoner of the Earth plane. We say prisoner because the Earth is one of the lowest vibrations in all of the life forms existing in the Creation. Yet, everything in your Inner-world is working to free you in your outer world, so you may rise above the `Earth illusion` and continue on to your `Higher consciousness` (God-self).

Be at peace with this Truth. By paying attention through your instincts, you will learn what your dreams are teaching you, and by exploring your Inner-world you will discover who you are and then your True self will illuminate all your experiences in this life. While learning to believe only that which you see and experience directly, you will create your freedom from others' intentions to manipulate your consciousness.

ASTRA

ASTRA CHANNELING
EMOTION/ENERGY--NOVEMBER 28, 2001

ASTRA: I welcome you all here! You are all receiving the light of love from your own heart, and you are experiencing your Light in the physical plane through experiencing your emotions. Your emotions are expressing the love that you desire, the love that you seek, and the love that you are. Although within the emotional body there is great turmoil there is also great realization (Light), at the same instant; for wherever there is darkness there is Light. Therefore, whatever is taking place within your emotional body at any given moment, whether it be dark, whether it be a happy emotion or a sad emotion, you are in a learning experience (you are in a process) in which you are always in connection with the `Higher` self….(through your emotional body).

The human consciousness is in sleep-state in truth and, therefore, you are unaware of the power of the emotional body. Many physical Be-ings feel that the emotions are an annoyance (burden), so they work to block their emotions. Many Be-ings bury their emotions because they believe their emotions are detrimental and will cause them trouble in their lives-or will block them from achievements in the physical plane. Therefore, they see emotion as a weakness. Be-ings are fearful of how they are seen by others and they do not allow themselves to express their emotions-for fear of damaging their created image of self (Ego).

Through hiding the emotions, the **Light within the heart is hidden from others and the God-self is blocked**. This happens because it is difficult for you in the physical plane to acknowledge that you are all `ONE` energy and that you are all that exists in truth and, therefore, all that you need you can supply for yourself. This Truth is difficult for your egos to absorb, which creates your seeking recognition from that which is outside of you....and this act always reflects back to you the illusion and, consequently, your True self is then hidden. When you are not expressing your true feelings (your emotions) with the people in your life (the expression that is of the `One` which you uniquely possess), you suffocate. The act of putting out your inner flame will always take place when you are feeling powerless and isolated within your circumstance.

Consequently, your emotions then manifest as false and untrue. At this present time on the Earth plane, people have lost the ability to recognize a true emotion versus a fabricated one. Many Be-ings can now laugh, or cry, not because the feeling is felt but rather because they search for the perfect expression which they believe might be required in any given situation. It is the illusion that is being experienced through man/woman in the physical world and it only focuses on outcome (what should you show in order to get what is desired). This is the short cut that most humans have learned to take, which robs them of True emotion. You have always been capable of these false emotions although they are now becoming more prominent in your earth reality. Why is this so? Man/woman in their sleep-state experience forgetfulness and cannot remember how to let go of the mind in order to feel the emotion. Instead they automatically disconnect from the True emotional reality of the moment....and a True experience is then lost.

Why does this manifest in your material world? Through your technology you get information quickly, and you receive images that resemble stories you have grown up with and continue to watch in your movies and TV shows. Therefore, world events do not feel real - they feel like a story that is happening to other people which you have never and will never encounter in your life….as you believe you live in <u>secure</u> isolation. Pure fantasy is what directs your emotions here; this is how feelings have become a means of avoiding truth and avoiding pain, while strongly believing through your Ego the illusions that shield you from taking <u>any</u> responsibility for the negativity that manifests in your world.

This is what is meant by Sleeping Be-ings; the human has become a sleep walker - he/she walks through life wearing blinders as a fearful horse does when moving towards safe ground….and so man does when he/she is blinded to the Truth. This lifetime for all Be-ings is a powerful one because man/woman must awaken and can only awaken through the emotional body. It is difficult for many Be-ings to hear what has just been said for they do not understand what it means to put so much trust in the emotions. I say to them: God lives within your emotional body--for the feeling self holds the memory of the Creator and the unconditional love that has created life itself.

Q. How then does a Be-ING become aware of his/her true emotions?

ASTRA: When living within periods of time in isolation. When I speak of isolation, I speak of being alone with yourself, living in the company of your Whole self. This means living with your physical self and your Inner-self (the feeling self) that is deeply connected to your thought process and, therefore, it is the emotional-self that works to evaluate the true reality of your physical life. Through the emotional reactions that are taking place in every moment you spend alone, discovery of the true self becomes possible. I am not saying here that man/woman must separate from one another so they can feel emotion, I am saying that time alone is required in order to find the way back to feeling (true-emotion).

Q. What is true emotion?

ASTRA: It is `feeling` emotion, in that the feelings are powerful and demonstrate clearly what is being experienced in the moment. Is it a truthful moment or is it a lie in Truth? These questions are answered when there is a deep connection to seeing and feeling the reality of the moment. Many spiritual Be-ings test their belief systems through pulling their energy back from others for a period of time-in order to make room for the `Higher` self (feeling-self) to evaluate their present situation. This saves them valuable time for it provides answers that only their emotions can determine for them.

Know the self, for you cannot know the Creator until you know yourself....and you cannot know yourself until you feel yourself from the depth of your Be-ING; to know that which is bright and light and joyful within you....and that which is dark and fearful within you...by feeling the love and the hate that you hold within your emotional body, is how you create your reactions to the events in your life. This is when you can evaluate that which would torture the soul and that which would nurture the soul. Here you are <u>truly</u> serving the self....by not following the herd of sleep walkers into the darkness of illusion.

Let us now take your next question. You may begin.

Q. Lately, I have been creating a situation where I have this need to be right. It is just that I THINK that I am right. How can I face it, how can I heal this need to be always right?

ASTRA: You think you are right, but you do not feel that you are right. Is that what you are saying?

Yes, it is just a need to be right.

ASTRA: When you are saying the need to be right, you are then, of course, speaking about fearing being wrong, because you would not need to be right if you didn't fear that you were wrong. Do you follow what we say? This is where the need to be right comes from. The fear that you are always wrong; and the fear that you are going to be rejected is what makes you, through the ego; fabricate a feeling of rightness around your energy. Now others would see you as right, for your energy strongly demonstrates the power of being right. There are consequences for this. When the need becomes too great, then you will become argumentative with other Be-ings while always pushing the image of being right. The greatest consequence here is that you will not allow yourself to listen, so therefore, you cannot take in new information. What lies underneath this feeling is a desperate fear of rejection, fear of not being loved….is at the core of this need. You are operating out of lack which creates fear; while in truth you have nothing to fear. The truth is: you are both right and wrong….you are within knowing and within not knowing. You teach and you learn, both in every moment. Everyone is with wisdom and with ignorance. Within every living Be-ING all of this exists. You are all `One energy,` in Truth, each connected to the other.

While in body, man/woman is struggling for the power to understand his/her true purpose in order to serve the Whole, in Truth. Yet, the ego in man turns this into the illusion of gaining power through serving the self with the material, which he manifests through greed. Here is where your true suffering lies....for the material cannot create Love - only you can create Love in your world when connecting to your truthful emotional body.

Q. I really want to ask if healing the self could come from other sources; maybe come from other planetary Be-ings or Alien worlds?

ASTRA: We have said before that all is One and, therefore, the `One` is eternal. There are many levels of life in Creation and the Earth is but one level. There are existing other planets and other Be-ings; which are all of the `One energy` as well - Vibrating their powerful wisdom into the Whole.

We shall describe this in a visual you can easily understand. Visualize the God force as a giant tree, with many branches. The trunk of the tree is wide and goes deep into the earth where its roots travel and gather water for its survival within the physical. Its branches are many and they rise far above the ground reaching for the sky. God is the trunk and you are the branches reaching for the experiences-that will bring you the lessons which teach you of your God-self. Here is the sacred reason that one is many times buried beneath or near a tree.

A great variety of Be-ings that exist in the many universes are the branches of the tree which reside where there is much light and where the heavens rain upon those who touch the sky; therefore, these Be-ings are of a very High consciousness. They are the Aliens that we speak of who serve the Highest consciousness – and - are in service to the branches that are hidden from the sun, where there is not much light reaching them creating the consciousness to be of a denser vibration.

Earth is where the branches are in the middle of the tree. Therefore, human intelligence is of a lower vibration while the Alien branches are at the top of the tree, connecting to the `Highest` intelligence. These Aliens work to serve the Earth and protect the Galaxy. They heal the damage that is created through the ignorant choices that are made on the Earth plane (due to sleep-state) which creates and dominates the consciousness that now exists on the earth.

Q. What does this mean?

ASTRA: The Light exists within everything; it exists within all darkness. The Light can stand on its own, where the dark cannot. The dark requires the Light to sustain it. Therefore, while you are in physical body on the Earth Plane, you are learning and growing, and you will begin to open the heart and you will then bring into the earth more Light. Becoming discerning, you let in only that which is connected to Love and you serve only through Love. You do this while within knowing that Love is the only True `healing energy` in all of Creation. Your life's work then becomes clear- to preserve the Creation. When your intentions are pure and your heart is open, than your love is for all that exists within the Creation; this is when you can work and draw in positive energies from beyond your planet-which can assist in serving the healing of your planet and all of the Be-ings upon it.

Begin now by healing your own emotional body. The Higher entities we speak of have healed their emotions and are able to view the truth within any situation-through connecting to and absorbing the emotions of others. Understand how important it is then that your emotions are within Truth rather than illusion, for truth is directly connected to Love....and herein lays the reason why: only Truth can set you free.

We shall now ground Anna. Be in Truth and you shall be `Free` to love in Truth.

ASTRA

ASTRA's Class-August 3, 2000
Healing the Inner Child
Why We are More Inclined Towards the
Negative Than the Positive

ASTRA: Welcome to all. You are receiving light from the God plane. You are receiving guidance and love, in that you are sharing in these moments. You are sharing a reality.... while within the illusion. This may seem extremely awkward because it may feel as though you are in the reality speaking of an illusion or a desired reality. Yet, the truth is that you are speaking of the True reality; you are describing a reality that is....and you are describing it from the illusion that exists within the physical plane. Know that you are loved and you are guided to recognize that within the illusion you are seeking the Truth....for when the heart is open to receive the Light that exists in the moment, you come into the reality of your God-consciousness (Truth).

You may now ask your questions and we shall assist you. You may begin.

Q: I am working on my inner child. Would you give me some insight on what my child may need to help her heal?

ASTRA: The insight that you can retain at this moment is that your Inner-child is the part within your Be-ING that holds all your fears and confusion. While you are within your present moment and experiencing a blockage, (that creates within you a negative emotion), you must concentrate and follow your instincts, and ask yourself this question: **Why am I feeling this way?**

"I do not choose to feel this way, therefore, how am I choosing it?" You on one hand may say: "I did not choose it and I don't want it."

Here you are experiencing the duality in which you live.

Duality exists within your consciousness, for there is a part within every Be-ING that doesn't want to choose what it is that they are choosing. This occurs because you have chosen out of habit. It is a choice made out of an old pattern which has been deeply ingrained within the consciousness.

First, when you are battling with these feelings, the choosing out of habit must be realized. Therefore, next, you are to question: where did your choice to feel this way come from? If you have difficulty finding out the deepest reason for your feelings, you might at first find a surface reason.

You might say: "I chose this because that person reminded me of someone from my past, someone I used to be friends with and that is why I'm feeling this way."

You should always question yourself to the deepest level that you can go. Begin by keeping notes-writing down your feelings. This is an excellent way to work alone when one is working by oneself and does not have a helper in this path of work.

A good and excellent method is: at the end of the day write down all the feelings that you remember.

"I went to the grocery store and I felt like - this - I had a phone call and I felt this - way. I was alone for three hours, and these are the thoughts and feelings that came up."

Keep a log and at the end of the week, read the whole week. You will then begin to see similarities in your emotional experiences. When you see a similarity zero in on it….and trace it back to your childhood. This is a good beginning for all of you here. All Be-ings can work in this – way - it is extremely helpful, for the root of all confusion felt in your Outer world is rooted in your Inner-world (the childhood).

We will now take the next question.

Q: I don't think it's fair that we have to deal and manifest so much negativity when we are capable of doing much more. We can draw in the positive to us by thinking or living in the positive. I don't know why we are more inclined to be negative than positive.

ASTRA: The reason you are so well equipped is as a spiritual Be-ING you are one with the Creative Force, your True identity. Therefore, you are totally equipped to live in the light and to live in the manifestation of the good….to live in the positive. What is truly manifesting here is that you have forgotten that you are a spiritual Be-ING; for your Ego is in sleep-state….which separates you from the memory of your True identity.

You are fallen angels, as you have been called, and you have come into the physical world….you have come into body without the memory of your True identity. At your beginning (as physical Be-ings) you began experimenting with the negative forces….and experiencing creating through darkness. Working within this limited vibration you became trapped. You were trapped through your being seduced by the physical, material objects that you created. Because you began through this limited way of creating (physical manifestations)….you believed that your creations were a reality as they took form within physical matter. Form within matter creates a physical substance....which works to create the belief that these material manifestations were your True reality. When this took place you were no longer within the reality of your God-consciousness.... you were rather in loss of memory of your True self.

You are lost within Ego-consciousness, and this did not happen overnight....this did not happen in one lifetime.... this has been taking multitudes of lifetimes to manifest. Earth has been within this cycle for multitudes of your earth years....therefore, the Be- ings upon it have been gradually sinking more and more into <u>forgetfulness</u>. It is not an individual person that we are speaking of, or an individual entity that is lost in darkness. It is all of creation in the physical that is lost in darkness (perception), lost in the Ego-consciousness,which creates through loss of memory.... existing only within darkness.

Even though you create in darkness the Light is still present, for the `Light` is who you are in <u>Truth</u>. All of creation is still one with the Creator. Creation is still functioning out of Love and Light. Therefore, it is only this part of the consciousness, (Ego) that is functioning through the darkness and limiting the True power which exists within the human consciousness.

This is very difficult to visualize and very difficult to explain in material terms; yet, we will work to guide you in order for you to understand it more clearly. You are in the physical body and at the same instant you are with God....you are with the Creator....you are with the `One` why? Because the Mind of the `One`-is your mind....the Heart of the `One`-is your heart. You are energy of color and sound that vibrates within the Light....you are all in `One` with the Creative Force. You never left the Creator....you never separated from the Creator in Truth.

To see how this is so, visualize your energy as a stream of light....just as when you look up at your sky and you see a lattice of light in the sky.... descending streams of Light coming down into the earth. These streams of Light truly are a reflection of God, reflecting into this physical manifestation called Earth; and you are these `streams of `Light` reflecting God Light through your physical body. This is why we say to you, the earth is an illusion, for you are in the earth which is not your `True reality` (home). Yet you are the reflection of <u>wisdom</u> and all <u>knowledge</u> streaming into the physical Earth plane. You may see this Light as strands of DNA for they are the connecting vibrations that are now missing from your physical body and need to be connected through the spinal cord-where they will then ignite the memory of your True Identity.

As Be-ings you have enjoyed connecting with the physical substances that have been illuminated through these streams of Light. Now (in this moment) you are intermingling, feeling, touching, sensing, and smelling many physical and emotional sensations throughout your physical body-as directed towards you through these streams of Light. The reason this is happening is for you to awaken the True self....which realizes the Higher-consciousness.

Remember the creation is continuous....it is always moving and expanding; although, at this time, your streams of Light no longer reflect the One (God). Your ability to create through the Ego became so joyful and expansive that your Light moved away from the Higher realms and into the physical Ego-consciousness, where your-`Light`- is now <u>trapped</u> in the Earth plane. The exploring of the Ego took place in order for you to become more intimate with your physical creations. Therefore, in order to enjoy this Ego illusion, your wisdom of the Creation (Creator) was cut off....and your focus now mainly exists in the physical material experience, (the illusion).... hence, your physical entrapment.

Your present reality is that you are trapped within an illusion....and by cutting off the consciousness of the God-self you do not remember that you <u>are in</u> the illusion. You are now in `sleep-state` and the illusion is your <u>only</u> reality. Here exists the reason why you are on this journey....why you came into this Earth creation; you came in to find and explore your God-self. You are <u>now</u> beginning the work that creates your <u>freedom</u>....freedom to seek and find the `Higher` consciousness (Truth).

All has been created by the Creator. All the streams of consciousness (within man and woman) are within the `Light` of the creative force. The consciousness that created your entrapment is the Ego. Your missing streams of `Light`(strands of DNA) must be discovered through the <u>mind</u>....and connect to the <u>physical body</u>. Bringing you into your God-consciousness, where you are `always` one with all of Creation....`always` in bliss....`always` exploring within unconditional love. Your loss of memory of your God-self requires you to find that <u>closed</u> door within your mind (which separates you from God) and to <u>open</u> that door TO THE LIGHT once more.

Every Be-ING on the earth plane is here in order to learn how to open the heart. Love holds the description of your True-identity and is speaking of your Godliness. Most Beings on the earth plane are blocked in the `Heart Chakra` where there exists great fear/confusion and misunderstanding which are created through the `ego perception` therefore, this does not permit the heart to open. Yet, sometimes the heart opens a little bit, and slams shut again. Other times it opens further and love manifests within the illusion; yet, not in its true nature, therefore, the heart shuts again.

The reality is the work must be continuous in order for the heart to open. How does the heart begin to open? The answer is by opening the heart to embrace yourself first; you must open to love yourself, and the only possible way to love yourself is to truly know yourself. Learn about yourself (to the depth of your Be-ING)....know when you are within ego, when you are in the illusion. Confront your darkness, giving yourself the power to walk into the Light. Through these actions you will generate great love for your own Be-ING. The more love you show to your own Be-ING through this healing process, and discovery process, the more freedom to open your heart to others will manifests. Now the door will open. This is your path....it is taken in multitudes of ways, therefore, each Be-ING must find his/her own path to an <u>open</u> and <u>loving</u> heart.

Q: Was love designed as a tool in order to help us to open the heart?

ASTRA: Love is <u>what</u> you are, love is <u>who</u> God is, and love is your <u>True</u> identity. You are love and through your physical Ego-consciousness you can direct the love. Now you may <u>acknowledge</u> it as a tool for healing yourself. In other words, <u>acknowledge</u> that you are love, know that you are of the Creator and the Creator is Unconditional Love. <u>Acknowledge</u> that love exists within your own Be-ING, for it is the substance (energy) through which you came into being. <u>Acknowledge</u> that when love is corrupted it is being experienced through your Ego-consciousness and, therefore, it is not pure, and cannot be unconditional. Yet, love shows itself to your ego and through your ego in many ways. Honor the love that comes through the Ego as well. In order to heal the parts of your ego which are pulling away from the love and gravitating towards darkness and pain, greed and judgment you must consciously say to yourself-I can and I will heal through my Ego.

Ego is now all that you truly EXPERIENCE within your conscious mind in your earthly world. Gently guide your ego into accepting the love at whatever level it can accept. Use your will to direct the love that passes through the Ego.... then consciously work to eliminate the darkness from your ego perception. When you are working on yourself, going deep within, you are facing your darkness by utilizing the power of <u>Love</u> to go there. This act of love helps your <u>Ego</u> to penetrate its false belief system. In order to heal through your Ego-consciousness, your ego must feel loved enough to accept the healing. Therefore, love yourself as you are now in this moment with all your darkness and Light.

Seek your peace in Love.

ASTRA

Dream-Insert: Aliens in Our World

The following teachings are from a dream I, Anna, had - Confirmed by ASTRA.... For its truth content.

Anna Speaks:

Are there "ET's" among us, above us and around us? Yes!

The statement above may be a frightening thought for some people because the unknown is a mystery and its content could be anything from bliss to horror. Yet, for those of us who are on a spiritual path, (who are continuously exploring the unknown within ourselves), this concept is exciting and generates hope for a way out of the tangled web of illusion. The illusion that we on the path have come to know is the foundation for all separation and pain.

Maybe you believe that this topic is for fiction only, yet it is more truthful than that. Why is it so hard to believe that we are not the only living beings within the Mufti- Universe's? Perhaps because we live in a vacuum, an isolated area of our own universe billions of miles away from other life forms. This isolation is not an accident, this was intended, for we are an experiment, our home Earth is an experiment. It is likened to a single cell in a test tube; where a desired outcome is hoped for, yet caution is always taken against an unfortunate dangerous outcome. Therefore, other life forms (Aliens') are monitoring us in order to protect us from an unfortunate outcome. That is why we are contained and we live within the consciousness of duality....which helps to insure our survival in the physical plane.

We have been crossbred with galactic memories that are imprinted on our DNA. We are Star Energy, which means we came out *of the belly of the Creator, for whom we call by many different names, `God,` `The Christ,` `Mohammad` and `Abraham` etc., Universal thought is a collaboration of all these given names for the Creator, meaning: All-in-One. This brings us to the concept of `ONE,` which has been injected into our test tube called Earth, (injected by Aliens of a Higher-consciousness who are running this experiment), injecting into our DNA this powerful element of <u>Truth</u> in order to assist us in creating our freedom. Yet so few of our human population have connected to this germ of Oneness…. that now the Aliens are working overtime to find the cure for what is known as <u>Illusion</u>. Illusion which is so powerful, it continues to block out the <u>truth of Oneness</u>, while <u>denying</u> us the ability to free and raise our own consciousness.*

The Earth as a `Galactic-experiment` has become negative and is now becoming more dangerous for our Galaxy and beyond. This present danger is why we are being visited by other worlds, and why people on the earth have had Alien experiments done on their bodies. The cure needs to be found.

"Free choice" was given to us here on earth in order to evaluate our intelligence and behavior, while measuring our level of consciousness. It also works to aid the human entity to move quickly away from danger when necessary. There are numerous ways that we humans have abused this gift of free choice, and have distorted our individual connection to the `Truth of Oneness.` This distortion serves to empower our illusions….our fears, and creates our addictions to the material forces which our egos have created. Our first purpose for these material creations was to bring ease and comfort for maintaining the body and clearing out disease and impurities found on the Earth. We were meant to create a blissful, peaceful society in our Universe, where all visitors from other

Galaxies could come and rest, (replenish the-self), before returning to their complex missions for maintaining and holding the Galactic balance. On the Earth they could be in human form enjoying the `Living Truth` within this manifested `Earth reality`....of peace and joy.

We talk about Alien ships, crop circles, and the council of space travel, about visitations from other worlds; not recognizing that these are programs created for correcting an experiment gone wrong....that is us (The Earth Experiment). Far too many of us are trapped in the material illusion and only seek full power over the Galaxy. These are the thought patterns that will ultimately destroy our Universe if not reprogrammed.

The question for all of us who are on the path of Oneness is: How do we mobilize the masses so we may affect a change that would (aspire to) raise the consciousness of the many, creating the desired outcome of a paradise.... here on Earth, serving our Galaxy?

The teachings in `Awaken` are our gift from the Highest Realm of consciousness which gives a clear description of the path to take for the raising of Human consciousness. The path to take describes how to redirect our intentions in order to protect the Earth through adding to her perfection....rather than stealing her beauty and power for selfish gain. Only when these teachings are able to be realized through our own experiences, will we truly be serving ourselves.... while living in the Truth of Oneness.

CHAPTER XII
EXERCISES FROM `ASTRA`
THE ANGELIC GUIDE

1. RAISING THE CONSCIOUSNESS
2. CHILDHOOD INVESTIGATIONS
3. DISCOVERING YOUR GIFTS

FIRST EXERCISE-RAISING THE CONSCIOUSNESS

By our learning to listen to our thoughts, we than can consciously choose our thoughts. Changing a negative thought, into a positive one releases the negative habit of judging the self and punishing the self for feelings of unworthiness.

Step 1: ASTRA Speaks:

Begin by consciously paying attention to your language and your inner thoughts. Practice changing a negative thought into a positive one. Do this always seeing yourself as deserving, and know that there is no <u>real</u> block to receiving that which you deeply desire. Therefore, when a negative thought rises, remember that the power of that thought will manifest into your world. Why is this so? As you have learned through these teachings, all of your thoughts manifest into the physical embodiment. <u>Your</u> <u>thoughts create your life.</u>

Step 2: Write Thoughts

<u>Example writing</u>: *"I am not getting this job! I know it because the interviewer looked at me in a way that clearly said he did not like me."*

<u>Changed Thought</u>: *"I had a good interview; I was intelligent and knowledgeable about the work required for this position. I feel confident that I will get this job."*

*As you continue to change your thoughts you will find that at first, you will have to change your thoughts constantly, practically in every moment....at first this will be hard to bear. Yet, as you continue to change your negative thinking.... negative thoughts will no longer have access to your mind. This may take a month or 6 months, but at the end of this time you will be free of negative thinking and negative language.

Step 3: Check Your Responses

<u>Keep a Diary</u>: Once a week write in your diary what positive things took place from your thinking in positive ways. When you change your <u>negative thinking</u> you will then have a <u>positive outcome</u>. Write down in your diary all the positive outcomes that manifested from the positive thoughts that you have created. Your confidence will build, by listing all the good that has come from your ability to examine your thinking....and you will then take back your power as the creator of your own life. Pay close attention to your language at this time. When you give a negative response to someone's comments, re-think quickly in that moment-and insert a positive response.

<u>Example</u>: *"My son is only 15 and he cursed at me in such vile language, that I was frightened, I thought next he would hit me.*

What I did than was cry, I sat in the corner like I was the child being punished."

A Negative Response: "*O my dear, you should have called the police and had him put in jail. He is a bad seed and you must not allow yourself to be threatened by him. The way you acted was wrong and now he will continue to frighten you.... only, because he knows that he can. You better get someone to straighten him out.*"

A Positive Response: "*I am so sorry to hear that, I know how much you love your son, and this was very hard for you to experience. Don't be so hard on yourself for being shocked in that moment, who wouldn't be shocked? Only you know what might be bothering him, so I cannot tell you what to do, but I will say this, please talk to your son and try to find out what's wrong, if you can. He loves you! You know that, so something must have gone wrong in his life. Maybe you can get him the help that he needs. Whenever you want to talk I will be here for you. Try not to worry about him hating you. Don't suffer that thought, that's not what this is about. No matter what happened he is still your son.*"

*Practicing living in your Higher-consciousness on a daily bases changes your life, changes your heart enhancing your creativity.

Pay attention to your feelings and how they change when you have a positive thought....and when you speak in positive language. Note the change in your feelings every time you change the thought, and then write the new feelings in your book of positive responses.

Second Exercise-Childhood Investigations

*When you are investigating your inner world you come face to face with your Child-self. Here is where you can discover how you lack self-love.... and why you hide yourself within many disguises. You are doing this in order to fit and align yourself to receive acceptance from others. Why do you do this? Within the child's memory of the past is where hatred for the self-resides, therefore, healing the inner-child must be your priority. This is the only path to self-realization, and freedom from adopted `Ego perceptions` which have created the foundation on which you have built your life.

Step 1: Book of Memories
List all remembered experiences from the earliest age on to the present time: in which you have felt pain or embarrassment, anger, fear, and or confusion.

Alongside of each memory write how you felt in that moment. Your feelings may or may not be remembered, but they are important for your understanding of the self, so work to piece together the event.... and your reaction (external and internal) to it. By doing this, you will begin to see how you felt one way, and reacted in another.

Children naturally work to protect themselves from hurt, and abandonment, and, therefore, do not follow through on their inner feelings in the moment.... but rather hide feelings.... in order to stay safe (physically or emotionally). Many times the level of confusion is so great....that the child does not know what to feel, or do, and withdraws into a shell for self-preservation, or becomes aggressive and demanding....in order to receive what he/she fears is being withheld (love/protection). The latter is the healthier choice, for this child is learning how to give what he needs to him/herself. The former leaves this child to live life through the mind…. rather than taking the physical actions required in the moment. This is the foundation/ path, where many artists develop while living through their imagination. Therefore, both former and latter experiences can work to provide a positive path (once discovered).

Step 2: Create a List

On the list that you will write use only key words heard from the past that have affected your child-self in a negative way.

Example:
1. You're fat!
2. Be quiet! You talk too much.
3. What are you laughing at?
4. You look smart, but you are not smart.
5. You are so selfish!
6. Nobody likes a show off.
7. You smell funny!
8. Give that toy to your sister, it's not for you.
9. That's right, Santa gave you coal because your bad.
10. Nobody could ever love that face!

After writing your list of remembered hurtful words, write opposite each word how they are still affecting you in some form in your present life.

Example:	As a result:
You're fat!	*I always feel fat.*
Talk too much	*I am nervous when speaking*
What are you laughing at?	*I laugh quietly*

Step 3: Discoveries

After doing these exercises, <u>write</u> what you have <u>discovered</u> about yourself. State what your child-self has taken in as the truth about you, which you now understand to be an untruth. <u>List</u> these discoveries, and next to them <u>write</u> how you will change yourself.... in order to reflect what you have learned is the <u>real Truth</u> about you.

<u>Example:</u>   <u>New belief:</u>
My feeling fat is just a feeling   *I love my body*

*As you make your discoveries, continue to write them in your book. Read them every night before you retire. This is how your inner-child will hear them and take them to heart. Remember, that all your feelings from childhood are embedded in every cell of your body. In order to create new and positive feelings that replace the negative ones, you must <u>repeat the positive</u>. Always remembering that the Ego believes, and trusts, in all that is repeated numerous times. It is the repeating of the positive which will <u>shift your consciousness.</u>

THIRD EXERCISE-DISCOVERING YOUR GIFTS

Discovering your gifts is easier than you might think. Believe it or not your gifts are developing through your childhood experiences (good and bad). All that you <u>are</u> and <u>all</u> that you have <u>experienced</u> expresses your creativity, in many, many ways.

<u>Example:</u> If you are forced as a child to perhaps clean your room every day, and wash the dishes every night, you begin to find ways to either enjoy what you are doing, or

escape the doing, thinking in creative ways to do either. As you begin to examine these times you will clearly see a gift developing.

Step 1: Create Book: "Finding my gifts": Earliest discoveries List gifts found in childhood

<u>Example</u>: *When I was 7 years old and I had to go to my room (because I didn't listen to my mother), I would play music and pretend that the music would push out my mother's voice and all I would hear than was a happy sound. This became a creative time for me, for each time I was punished I began to write my own songs, songs, which described how beautiful and good I was. After a while I shared my songs with my family at parties, and they all thought.... how wonderful and funny my songs were.*

<u>Realization</u>: *This is where my gift of humor was discovered.*

<u>List findings as follows</u>:
1. <u>Childhood event remembered</u>:
2. <u>Realization of gift</u>:

*Out of a tragic experience you can realize a gift as well. When you become inventive in ways that will protect you from harm, ways that will bring you joy, that will many times become your greatest gift in later life.

The trauma that Anna had brought Anna the gift of `ASTRA.` Anna has dedicated her life to sharing her gift (creating her joy).
<u>Example</u>:
1. <u>Childhood event remembered</u>:

When I was 12 years old my father began to have rage all the time, he would yell at me and my brother for speaking at the dinner table.... and would throw food at us, or silverware. I got hit with a fork in the corner of my eye once, and my father blamed me for making him mad, saying, "If you boys would listen than I wouldn't have to get angry, this is what happens when you don't pay attention!"

Step 2: Realization of Gift

I possess a very calm way of handling myself with excitable people. There was always something in me that wanted to help those who had emotional struggles, when trying to handle their anger. I became an `anger therapist.` I see now that my gift came out of my fear, and my love both, for my father.

*As you continue to do this exercise you will realize, that the memories that stay strong in the recalling of your past-- hold volumes of information which confirms all that is <u>True</u> in your nature, all that is strong and good in <u>your personality</u>, as well as....all that has been <u>damaged</u> through the experiences of the past....through the `Child-self.`

As written above, this boy felt compassion for his father.... along with his fear of his father's anger. This aided him in developing his gift for helping others. Here is where you can clearly see how this experience helped him to find a way to create a positive solution. Although, the experience could have turned out differently through the child-self, for it could have created a block to self-love as well.... coming from the child's deep fear, and anger towards the one he loves.

Fear is what blocks love, and children possess a great deal of fear naturally. Therefore, they are in need of positive guidance from those who are able to protect them from over obsessing with their feelings of fear.

Do the exercises in this order and when you get to exercise 3, you will be prepared to find where the gifts you have <u>realized</u> came from. Also you will be prepared to discover the <u>hidden gifts</u> that you have....which have been blocked from you through the fear held in your inner-child

<u>How to find your hidden gifts</u>:
Keep a diary of experiences that shut you down, experiences that had frightened you in the past, all the remembered <u>traumatic</u> experiences.

<u>Example</u>:
A 12 year old girl is at the public pool with her friends.... and for the first time she is going to jump into the pool from the lowest diving board. When she does this, she slides to the bottom of the pool on a slopping wall....and is disoriented for a moment or two. Yet, she finds her way to the top: only to see the young man who is the lifeguard, screaming at her, saying, *"You could have killed yourself." You are not allowed to dive anymore GET OUT OF THE POOL!*

<u>Result</u>:
The girl was shocked at what happened because she was not aware that she could have been killed. This child never went back into the pool. She never was able to trust herself in the water again.

Reality:
This is a <u>false</u> fear, planted by a fearful lifeguard. His fear is what created his anger, and he blew his fear out of reality and created a <u>traumatic</u> experience for this child. His response to her joyful, first dive, is what devastated the young girl.

Remedy:
No matter how old this girl is today, the remedy is to go to the pool and take lessons in swimming and diving. There is a gift here that can be discovered, which will free her from limiting herself in life. Because her love of the water was blocked through fear, it blocked her <u>trust</u> for all that she loves in her life. Now, no matter what form the love takes (in life) it is being directed through fear.

Outcome:
Learning to reconnect to her love of the water is what will dissolve the fear which is blocking her from finding and connecting to the love that exists in her life. Here the greatest gift is discovered….the gift that frees many blocks all at once. All the blocks to love created from this past experience will then be resolved, and will no longer block her trust in what she loves.

The Work:
Dig into the places where you find the experiences that shocked or paralyzed you when you were growing up in this lifetime. All your traumatic experiences (remembered) large or small….through writing all that you remember in your diary….and then work to face these fears head on. This is how you will take your power back from the negative outcome. By releasing yourself from a damaging memory that holds so

much pain and or confusion....you will create the freedom to live in your <u>True</u> nature, (which is the goal).

The <u>goal</u> is: To discover all your gifts. Search the self to find your gifts and then create your life through them. Living through your <u>God</u> given gifts will produce a meaningful and productive life experience.

Within your exploration of Self you are blessed....take this journey in love and peace. ASTRA